EGYPT
UNCOVERED

EGYPT
UNCOVERED

VIVIAN DAVIES AND RENÉE FRIEDMAN

STEWART, TABORI & CHANG
NEW YORK

CONTEN

First published in 1998 by British Museum Press
a division of The British Museum Company Ltd
46 Bloomsbury Street, London WC1B 3QQ

Published and distributed in the U.S. in 1998 by
Stewart, Tabori & Chang
a division of U.S. Media Holdings, Inc.
115 West 18th Street, New York, NY 10011

Distributed in Canada by General Publishing Company Ltd.
30 Lesmill Road, Don Mills, Ontario, Canada M3B 2T6

Egypt Uncovered is an international television coproduction by S4C (Wales).
Produced by John Gwyn Productions for S4C in association with Discovery Channel (USA) and La Cinquième (France).

Designed by Harry Green

ISBN: 1-55670-818-1
Library of Congress Catalog Card Number: 97-62390

Printed in Great Britain
by Butler & Tanner Ltd, Frome and London
Color separations by Radstock Reprographics

10 9 8 7 6 5 4 3 2 1

TITLE PAGE: Scene showing King Seti I (*c*.1294–1279 BC), Temple of Seti I, Abydos.

OPPOSITE ABOVE: Statue of Thutmose III (1479–1425 BC).

OPPOSITE BELOW: Vignette from 'The Book of the Dead', belonging to a man called Ani. Nineteenth Dynasty.

PREFACE

There is a huge popular fascination with the ancient Egyptians and their great civilization, but also a common misconception that there is little left to be discovered about them. Nothing could be further from the truth. The Nile Valley and its adjacent deserts continue to be enormously productive archaeologically. Important new discoveries, enhancing our knowledge and transforming our views, are being made on a regular basis, both in the field and in the laboratory; indeed with such frequency that even Egyptologists now struggle to keep pace and popular syntheses often lag far behind.

Focusing on some (by no means all) of the key archaeological sites in Egypt and the Sudan and on a number of representative scientific projects, this book reviews major aspects of ancient Egypt and Nubia in the light of the latest advances in knowledge and with the full collaboration of the experts concerned. It has been written to accompany a five-part television series – a co-production between S4C (Wales), Discovery Channel (USA) and La Cinquième (France) – which covers the same topics, in a refreshingly responsible but still accessible and entertaining way. Of late, ancient Egypt has been very ill-served in the media, with an alarming number of television programmes purveying bizzare and misleading nonsense, some of it masquerading as serious Egyptology. The public deserves better. The reality is so much more interesting, rewarding and exciting than the fantasy. Egypt's story is a celebration of human ingenuity and skills, of resilience and adaptability, and of truly gigantic achievements; the story of a people, with recognisable concerns and worries, seeking to understand and control their world and doing so, in their uniquely distinctive way, for over three thousand years. It is a tale with a surprising twist, as the remains of these very people are now making a contribution to the modern world in a capacity that goes well beyond their Egyptological relevance.

The book could not have been produced without the co-operation of a large number of institutions and individuals (see Acknowledgements). Special thanks are due to the officials of the Supreme Council for Antiquities of Egypt and the National Corporation of Antiquities and Museums of the Sudan respectively, who gave us every assistance in visiting sites and in taking photographs; to colleagues in the field and in various museums and other institutions, who allowed us generous access to their material; and to the staff of the Department of Egyptian Antiquities, British Museum, who have been enormously supportive. A good proportion of the photographs was taken by Peter Hayman and Jim Rossiter of the British Museum Photographic Service. The line illustrations were drawn or adapted by Claire Thorne of the Department of Egyptian Antiquities. The computer graphics are the work of 4:2:2 Videographics of Bristol. The book has been designed, with customary skill and flare, by Harry Green. The final editing and processing, done with commendable calm and efficiency, under unusually hectic conditions, have been the responsibility of Coralie Hepburn and Julie Young of British Museum Press.

VIVIAN DAVIES AND RENÉE FRIEDMAN

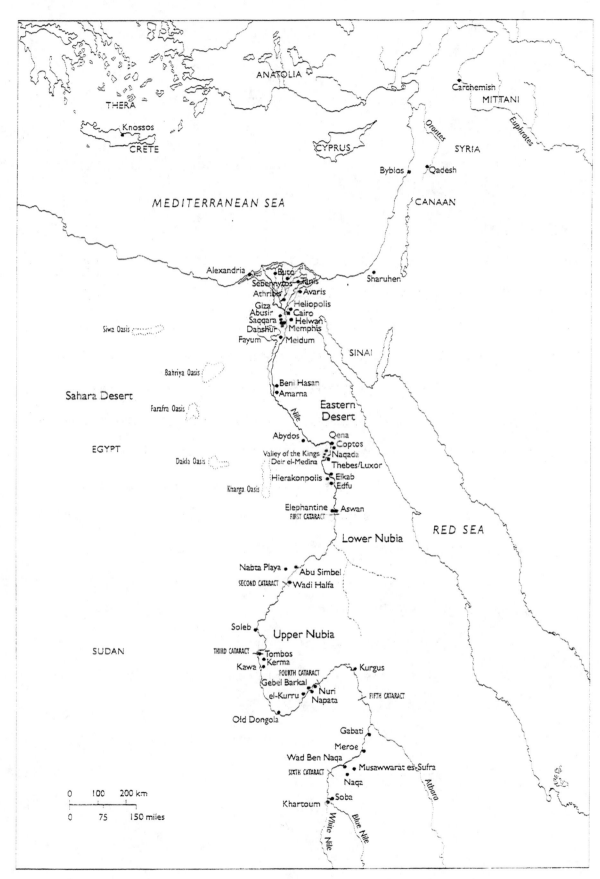

THERA

Knossos

CRETE

ANATOLIA

Carchemish

MITTANI

Euphrates

Orontes

CYPRUS

SYRIA

Byblos

Qadesh

MEDITERRANEAN SEA

CANAAN

Alexandria

Buto

Tanis

Sebennytos

Avaris

Sharuhen

Athribis

Giza

Heliopolis

Abusir

Cairo

Saqqara

Helwan

Dahshur

Memphis

Fayum

Meidum

Siwa Oasis

SINAI

Bahriya Oasis

Beni Hasan

Amarna

Sahara Desert

Eastern
Desert

Farafra Oasis

EGYPT

Abydos

Qena

Coptos

Valley of the Kings

Naqada

Dakla Oasis

Deir el-Medina

Thebes/Luxor

Hierakonpolis

Elkab

Edfu

Kharga Oasis

Elephantine

Aswan

FIRST CATARACT

RED SEA

Lower Nubia

Nabta Playa

Abu Simbel

SECOND CATARACT

Wadi Halfa

Soleb

Upper Nubia

SUDAN

THIRD CATARACT

Tombos

Kerma

Kawa

Kurgus

FOURTH CATARACT

Gebel Barkal

Nuri

el-Kurru

Napata

FIFTH CATARACT

Old Dongola

Gabati

Meroe

Wad Ben Naqa

Musawwarat es-Sufra

SIXTH CATARACT

Naqa

Abara

Khartoum

Soba

White Nile

Blue Nile

Nile

0   100   200 km

0   75   150 miles

8

ACKNOWLEDGEMENTS .

The authors are indebted to the many colleagues who have helped in various ways during the preparation of this book.

For sharing the fruits of their research and providing advice, access and information: Salah Mohammed Ahmed, Gus Alusi, Carol Andrews, Dorothea Arnold, Morris Bierbrier, Manfred Bietak, Charles Bonnet, Betsy Bryan, Joao Campos, Alfredo Castiglione, Angelo Castiglione, David Counsell, Deborah Darnell, John Darnell, Rosalie David, Anna-Maria Donadoni, Peter Dorman, Josef Dorner, Günter Dreyer, Arne Eggebrecht, Mohammed El-Saghir, Siddig Mohammed Gasm Elseed, Dina Faltings, Adel Farid, Richard Fazzini, Joyce Filer, Hans-W. Fischer-Elfert, Lesley Fitton, Joann Fletcher, Fawzy Gaballah, Ulrich Hartung, Ali Hassan, Fekri Hassan, Zahi Hawass, Fritz Hinkel, Hassan Hussein Idriss, Nasri Iskander, Peter Jánosi, David Jeffreys, Ray Johnson, Michael Jones, Tim Kendall, Mark Lehner, Jaromir Malek, Ian Mathieson, Theya Molleson, Mary Anne Murray, Paul Nicholson, Frank Norick, David O'Connor, Svante Pääbo, Richard Parkinson, Gillian Pyke, Stephen Quirke, John Ray, Mohammed Saleh, Romuald Schild, Louise Schofield, Sylvia Schoske, Abdeen Siam, Isabella Welsby Sjöstrom, Jeffrey Spencer, Rainer Stadelmann, Eddie Tapp, John Taylor, Jonathan Tubb, Patricia Usick, Miroslav Verner, Christopher Walker, Roxie Walker, Derek Welsby, Fred Wendorf, Helen Whitehouse, Dietrich Wildung, Jean Yoyotte, Christiane Ziegbo.

For invaluable logistical support and practical assistance: Jerry Baker, Caroline Biggar, Tony Brandon, Herma Chang, Reg Davis, Darrel Day, Bob Dominey, El-Tahir Adam El-Nur, Tony Fellowes, Sue Giles, Alan Goulty, Ben Green, John Hayman, Tim Healing, Mary Helmy, Romany Helmy, Ed Johnson, Jane Johnson, Howard M. Jones, Yarko Kobylecky, Judy McKeehan, Margaret Massey, Claire Messenger, Jim Putnam, David Rawson, Don Sloan, Christopher Sykes, Yolanda Sykes, Rowen Unsworth, Tania Watkins, Ken Wildsmith.

For making the project possible in the first place and for ensuring its successful conclusion: Huw Jones, Cenwyn Edwards and Ian Jones of Sianel Pedwar Cymru (S4C), Mike Quattrone, Steve Burns, Tomi Landis and Georgann Kane of Discovery Channel, and John Gwyn and his production team. On behalf of all the archaeological and scientific projects mentioned in this book, we thank the various funding and sponsoring agencies without whose support such work could never take place.

CHAOS AND

KINGS

hen the Greek historian Herodotus visited Egypt four and a half centuries before the birth of Christ, he was awestruck. 'The wonders were greater than those of any other land', he observed. There were pyramids taller than any man-made structure on earth. avenues of sphinxes, half-man, half-beast, colossal statues of long-dead pharaohs and all around the enigmatic symbols of Egypt's sacred writing. But two things intrigued him more than any other: Egypt's great antiquity and its most remarkable of rivers. the Nile.

Here along the banks of the Nile was a civilization that had flourished since time immemorial. To the ancients, Egypt was already ancient. Even the Egyptians. with the oldest recorded history in the world. had merged their beginnings with myth. It was a culture so old that its origins remained shrouded in mystery.

Herodotus said that Egypt was a land given to the Egyptians by the Nile. Its power to be 'contrary in nature' to all other rivers. by flooding its banks in summer. was a great puzzle to him and others after him. So it was to remain until Victorian explorers discovered its sources in two parts of East Africa. From Lake Victoria in present-day Uganda. the White Nile flows northward and is joined in the Sudan by the Blue Nile and Atbara River. both rising in the highlands of Ethiopia. After a journey of almost 3400 miles (5470 km). the river reaches the Egyptian Nile Valley to create an oasis 650 miles (1050 km) long through a pitiless desert. For its last 100 miles (160 km) it fans out into a broad delta plain before spilling into the Mediterranean Sea. Once a year, swollen by the summer monsoon rains in Ethiopia. the river flooded its banks, depositing nutrient-rich soil which the Egyptians called 'The Black Land'. Without it Egypt would be barren. With it, it was one of the most fertile regions on earth.

Left Colossal statues of Ramesses II (1279–1213 BC). Temple of Abu Simbel.

It is no surprise that the Nile had a profound effect on all aspects of the Egyptians' lives. Their calendar of twelve months, each of thirty days, the model for the one we use today, was based on it. They divided the year into three seasons: the time of the summer flood was called 'Inundation', 'Emergence' was when the water receded and crops could be planted, and the 'Dry Time' in the spring was the time of harvest. The division of the seasons meant the division of labour: the flooding of the land released a huge workforce that, while waiting for the waters to recede, could be employed on the major public building projects for which Egypt is so famous.

It seemed to Herodotus that there were no people in the whole world who gained from the soil with so little labour: 'the river rises of itself, waters the fields, and then sinks back again: thereupon each man sows his field and waits for the harvest.' But the Egyptians knew this was not always the case. Life on the Nile could be precarious, the climate could change dramatically and the river was unpredictable. Too high a flood and villages could be destroyed, too low a flood meant famine as the land turned to dust. Despite

Right Reaping grain. From the tomb of Mereruka, Saqqara. Sixth Dynasty. c.2330 BC.

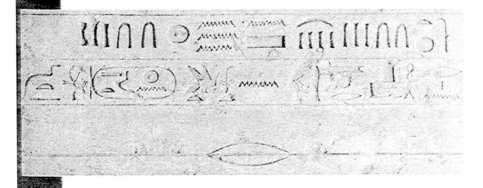

Left A stela marking the level of the Nile in year twenty-three of the king of Upper and Lower Egypt, Amenemhet III of the Middle Kingdom (1831 BC). The line through the oval at the bottom indicates the 'mouth' or height of the annual Nile flood waters. Taxes were levied according to the height of the inundation and the amount of land that would be watered and fertilized by it.

Above The conflict between Seth, the god of chaos and confusion, here depicted as a mythical creature with a pointed snout, and Horus, the falcon god of the sky, is reconciled in the person of the pharaoh, on whom they confer their blessings. From the temple of Ramesses II, Abu Simbel.

Opposite The delicate balance of the universe rested in the hands of the pharaoh in the form of his sister, the goddess *Ma'at*, seen here seated and wearing her characteristic feather headdress. From the temple of Ramesses II, Abu Simbel.

the fact that the Nile was more constant than any other of the world's great rivers, it is estimated that one Nile flood in five was either too low or too high.

The Egyptians called such events 'chaos' — the release of powerful forces which could disrupt their ordered world. To protect themselves from chaos, the Egyptians envisioned a ruler or pharaoh who was a living god, the earthly manifestation of Horus, the falcon ruler of the skies. Pitted against him was the unruly god of the desert, Seth, the harbinger of chaos, a force that needed to be controlled but could never be defeated. The reconciliation of the conflicting powers of order and chaos was the king's chief role. This delicate balance was so important to the Egyptians that they deified the concept as *Ma'at*, a goddess with the feather of truth on her head. *Ma'at* was the favourite daughter of the creator god and the wife of the god of wisdom. Since creation she had lived among humans on earth entrusted to the care of her brother, the pharaoh. It was his responsibility to look after her and to maintain her with justice, piety and, if need be, by force. Those who took good care of their sister were rewarded, but those who did not risked the vengeance of the gods.

This eternal conflict between order and chaos was a central concern of Egyptian civilization. The battle to harness the powers of nature, both cosmic and human, lies at the heart of Egypt's unique development. But the

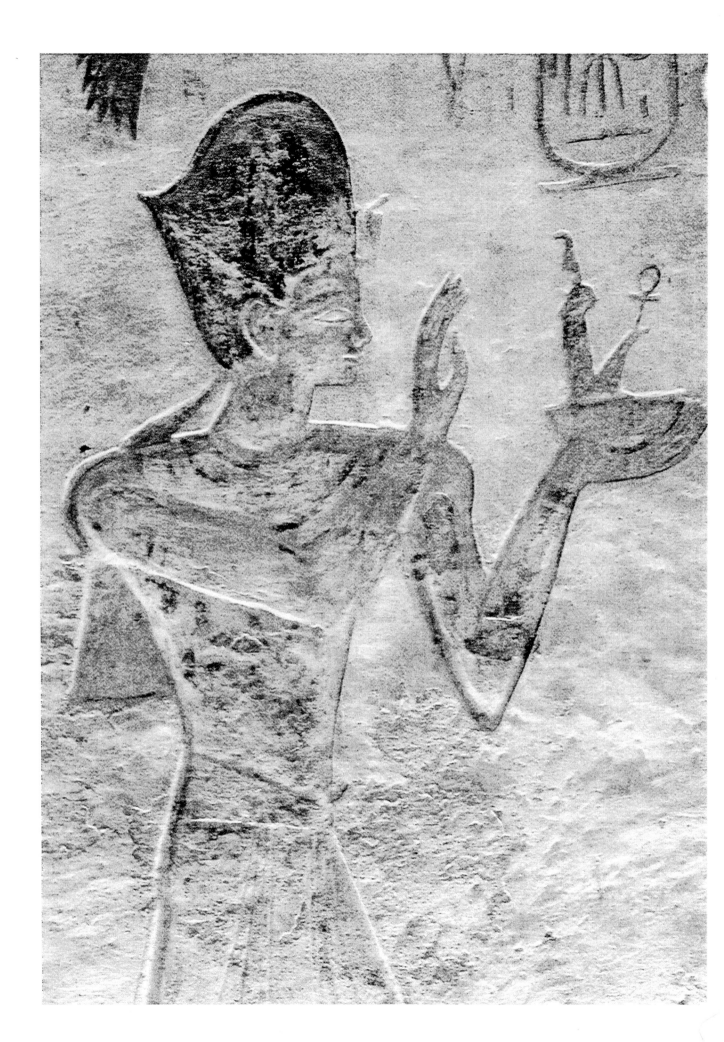

true story of how it all came about had vanished in antiquity and is only now reappearing with the help of the archaeologist's trowel.

In the twilight of Egypt's greatness around 300 BC, an Egyptian priest named Manetho began to compile a history of Egypt for his new monarch, Ptolemy, a Macedonian Greek successor to Alexander the Great. It was to be a complete history beginning with creation, and in it Manetho organized the pharaohs into thirty dynasties or royal families down to his own time. His history, however, has been preserved only in the works of later authors, who for the most part wished only to refute his claim of Egypt's vast heritage. Unfortunately these copies are often contradictory and rife with errors. Only tattered fragments remain of the detailed records Manetho must have examined, and we can only imagine the wealth of information they once contained. Yet a faint hint can still be gleaned from the walls of some of Egypt's most sacred places.

Above King-list from the temple of Ramesses II at Abydos, a similar version to that of his father, Seti I. Such lists, though selective in content, have been invaluable for building up an internal chronology for Egyptian history.

Chronology

Manetho organized his history of Egypt prior to the beginning of Greek administration into thirty dynasties of kings. Today the dynasties are grouped into broader kingdoms or periods of strong or weak government and cultural cohesion. Some dynasties overlap.

Predynastic and Dynasty 0	c. 4500–3100 BC	
Dynasties 1–2	c. 3100–2686 BC	Early Dynastic
Dynasties 3–8	c. 2686–2125 BC	Old Kingdom
Dynasties 9–10	c. 2160–2025 BC	First Intermediate Period
Dynasties 11–13	c. 2125–1650 BC	Middle Kingdom
Dynasties 14–17	c. 1750–1550 BC	Second Intermediate Period
Dynasties 18–20	c. 1550–1069 BC	New Kingdom
Dynasties 21–24	c. 1069–715 BC	Third Intermediate Period
Dynasties 25–30	c. 747–332 BC	Late Period
Macedonians/Ptolemies	332–30 BC	Greek administration
Roman emperors	30–642 AD	Roman/Byzantine administration

One thousand years before Manetho was born, King Seti I (1274–1279 BC) built a temple at Abydos dedicated to Osiris, the god of the dead. In a special 'Hall of the Ancestors' Seti is carved in exquisite low relief in the act of making offerings, while his young son, the future King Ramesses II, reads from a papyrus roll. The content of this document is carved on the wall before them – seventy-five of their revered royal ancestors listed in chronological order. The name of each king is encircled by a stylized coil of rope, a symbol signifying eternal protection that is called by Egyptologists a cartouche. It was the exclusive preserve of royalty: only the names of kings and queens were placed in a cartouche (the realization of this fact was critical for the decipherment of hieroglyphics in modern times). At the very end, Seti proudly adds his name to this continuous tradition of kingship spanning over 2000 years of Egyptian history. But where did it begin?

The earliest name in the list is King Menes, who, according to Manetho, founded Egypt's first dynasty, reigned sixty years, advanced his army beyond the frontiers of his realm and won great renown before being carried off by a hippopotamus. Yet Manetho, as Seti before him, knew that the beginning of Egyptian history was not the work of just one man. Before Menes, Manetho

Above Among the Spirits of the Dead who reigned before Menes were the falcon-headed Souls of Buto and the jackal-headed Souls of Hierakonpolis. Their presence was required to legitimize all royal functions throughout Egyptian history. Bronze. Late Period, after 600 BC.

relates, Egypt was ruled by the demigods also called the Spirits of the Dead, their names long forgotten. Among them were the falcon-headed Souls of Buto and the jackal-headed Souls of Hierakonpolis, the spirits of the deified dead kings of two towns in two very different parts of Egypt.

The Nile flows from south to north, and the narrow river valley in the southern portion of the country is thus called Upper Egypt. This is where Hierakonpolis is located. The flat alluvial plain of the Delta in the north was called Lower Egypt; here was Buto. The landscape of these two regions was strikingly different to the Egyptians, so much so that they considered their country as the 'Two Lands', each with its own heraldic flower, protective goddess, distinctive crown, royal title, capital and demigods, all brought together and unified through the power of the king.

Egyptologists have long pondered whether these dualistic divisions are merely manifestations of the Egyptians' love of symmetry, as seen in their art and architecture and ever apparent in the natural landscape. Or could there be encapsulated within them, fragments of half-forgotten fact about Egypt's beginnings? Archaeologists are now finding out. Remarkably, however, the story doesn't start along the banks of the Nile, but in the wilderness of the Sahara desert

Above Egypt was composed of the 'Two Lands', each with its own symbolic imagery. The Nile Valley of Upper Egypt was the land of the lotus, the kingdom of the White Crown, protected by the vulture goddess Nekhbet. The papyrus plant, the Red Crown and the snake goddess Wadjet symbolized the Delta in Lower Egypt. Coffin of Nesmut, c.950–900 BC.

Nabta Playa

The southwest corner of Egypt is the most arid place on earth. In this part of the Sahara desert less than one millimetre of rain falls each year, but it evaporates before ever hitting the ground. Yet here, for more than twenty years, an international team led by Professor Fred Wendorf of Southern Methodist University, Dallas, and Dr Romuald Schild of the Polish Academy of Sciences has been investigating the scattered remains of people who just may be the distant ancestors of the pharaohs. For the Sahara desert was not always so inhospitable. Some 10,000 years ago, Africa's summer rain belt shifted northward, increasing the amount of rain and allowing seasonal lakes or 'playas' to form in low-lying areas.

One such former lake is called Nabta Playa. Once the largest basin in the southeastern region of the Sahara, it lies about 60 miles (100 km) west of Ramesses II's famous temple at Abu Simbel. The water it collected from the summer rains provided the moisture for a grass-covered savannah-like plain shaded by drought-resistant trees such as acacias. On and off, for over 4000 years, it was the home for a nomadic people who learned to cope with this harsh and unpredictable environment. Now it is a remarkable laboratory for investigating how environmental stress contributed to social and cultural innovation.

Almost from the beginning the early inhabitants of Nabta had learned to herd cattle, perhaps the first to do so in all of Africa. They used them as renewable resources, living on their milk and blood rather than their meat. This made life in the desert possible. By 8000 years ago, a tightly organized way of life had developed which allowed them to remain in the desert all year long. Excavations in one lakeside village in 1974–7 by Wendorf and his team have revealed at least fifteen large oval houses originally made of sticks and reeds arranged in three parallel rows. Around the hearths and in nearby

Right Ten thousand years ago
the Sahara desert was a grassy
plain with numerous seasonal
lakes or playas filled by summer
rains. One of the largest lakes in
the southeastern region was
Nabta Playa.

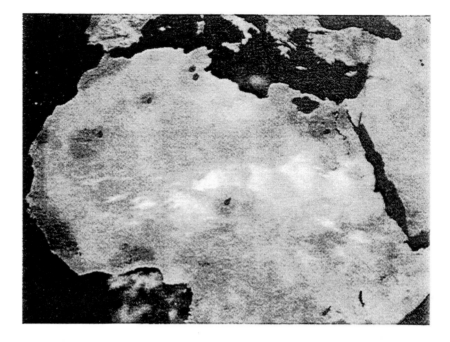

Below Excavation along the
former edge of the lake at Nabta
Playa revealed the remains of oval
houses with hearths, storage pits
and walk-in wells.

storage pits, some forty-four different varieties of grains, fruits and roots were recovered, as well as some of the oldest pottery in Africa. Three deep walk-in wells attest to a certain amount of community spirit in both their construction and use. Yet the key to the inhabitants' survival was the ability to predict when and if the rains would come, for after the last well ran dry, two days at most separated life from death.

In 1992 the team discovered the ingenious way in which the ancient Nabtans solved this problem. A circle of small upright stone slabs, only 4 m (13 ft) in diameter, looks like a miniature version of Stonehenge and was used perhaps in a similar way, but over 2000 years earlier. Co-director Romuald Schild explains how this, the oldest calendar ever found, worked:

Above Stonehenge in miniature. Co-director of the excavation Romuald Schild examines the world's earliest calendar.

'Four pairs of slabs in the circle are longer and set closer together than the others. These are called gates. Two pairs on opposite sides of the circle are aligned exactly north–south, while the other two are aligned at 70 degrees east of north. This direction points to the position of the sun on 21 June. That is the beginning of summer and was the beginning of the rainy season in this belt of Africa.'

Waiting for the summer solstice and counting the days until it rained must have been a serious business. But when the rains finally came, it was a time of celebration. Not far from the calendar circle, atop a high dune, is the place where the entire population must have gathered for the annual festivities. Over the years they left behind over 2 m (6.5 ft) of refuse and more cattle bones than anywhere else in the Sahara. It was a time for cattle slaughter, a rare and probably religiously charged event, both for consumption and also sacrificial burial, perhaps as offerings to the gods who brought the rain.

More intriguing still, the festival grounds also included a complex alignment of ten large standing stones and a series of thirty mounds crowned with huge stones, perhaps to mark the graves of important people. Remarkably, these stones, some weighing over one and a half tonnes, had been dragged into position from a quarry more than a mile away. Yet beneath one of these mounds was buried not a fallen ruler, but what appears to be an early sculpture. It is still possible to see how the sandstone was shaped: by making grooves and then using a wedge, the workmen were able to strike off the flakes at the exact points they wished. With its sharp edges and smooth faces, this sculpture is an impressive piece of stoneworking and according to Wendorf, 'may well mark the beginning of Egyptian fascination with working large stones'.

Above The sculpted stone found buried in a large pit beneath one of the mounds.

These monuments are the first evidence of the emergence of leaders who could command the building of large-scale public architecture. Their construction required a degree of skill, organization and commitment previously unknown at such an early date. It would seem that the stresses of survival in an unpredictable desert led to this unprecedented degree of social organization. For to survive in the difficult environment in which they lived, the people needed rulers who could make the life-or-death decisions on which their existence depended.

These remarkable early advances in technology and society seem, ironically, to correspond to the beginning of the end for these desert dwellers. Slowly the rains diminished and became more intermittent. Finally, around 6000 years ago, they ceased entirely and the Sahara desert became the barren waste it is today. What happened next is still unclear, but it is possible that when the last ruler made the decision to abandon the desert and led his organized band eastward to the life-giving waters of the Nile, they brought with them to Egypt many of those features that would soon distinguish this region from anywhere else on earth.

The Move to the Nile

The Nile waters that nourish and the silts that fertilize also bury and wash away. Whatever evidence there is for the interaction of the desert folks and the indigenous hunters and fishermen who lived along the Nile at that period is now deeply buried. We may never know exactly what happened, but within a short time, amazing things began to occur. Soon the first glimmerings of Egyptian civilization appear within the graves of the prehistoric, or Predynastic, inhabitants of the Nile Valley. In them are found some of the finest and most elegant pottery vessels ever produced in Egypt. Later came

Above Around 4000 BC some of the finest and most elegant pottery ever produced in Egypt began to appear in Upper Egyptian graves.

animal-shaped palettes for grinding cosmetics, carved out of stone from distant quarries. In the most wealthy and élite tombs were flint knives so expertly ground and flaked that they have never been equalled. They could only have been made by dedicated master craftsmen.

First discovered in 1895, these Predynastic graves reveal the long history of the ancient Egyptian belief in an afterlife into which the dead could take with them both their wealth and their status. The conspicuous consumption evident in the rich graves of a minority shows that already by 4000 BC there

Right Animal-shaped palettes of slate for grinding cosmetics. c.3300 BC.

Below Finely crafted flint knives. c.3600–3200 BC.

were the rulers and the ruled. No longer was the Nile Valley a land of hunters and gatherers. It could well be that the lessons learned earlier in the desert gave the Upper Egyptians the competitive edge against their neighbours and set them on the path that would ultimately lead to the birth of the Egyptian nation. But how they adapted these lessons and developed them into a distinctive civilization cannot be discerned in the graves alone. For the full picture, one has to investigate their settlements.

Hierakonpolis

The ancient site of Hierakonpolis, a Greek name meaning 'city of the falcon', was long venerated by the ancient Egyptians as the early capital of the Kingdom of Upper Egypt and the home of the falcon Horus, the patron god of kingship. The discovery a hundred years ago of rich caches of discarded temple furnishings on a low mound within the modern village seemed to confirm the ancient traditions about the site. But it was not until the American Expedition, formerly led by Dr Michael Allen Hoffman, took to the field

in 1978 that the true foundation of its importance started to emerge. A century ago, archaeologists thought that all that the desert surrounding the site contained was a plundered cemetery not worth exploring. Little did they know that hidden beneath its crater-pocked surface was a wealth of new information on one of the most significant chapters in Egyptian history.

Recent explorations have shown that by 3500 BC Hierakonpolis was the most important settlement along the Nile – a vibrant, bustling city already equipped with many features that would later come to typify Egyptian culture and form the basis of its economy. Stretching for over 2 miles (3 km) along the edge of the floodplain, it was a city of many neighbourhoods, filled with farmers, potters, craftsmen and officials.

In 1978 the Hierakonpolis Expedition uncovered the house and workshop of one particular potter who produced cooking pots for his neighbourhood clientele. He signed his pots by impressing a crescent-shaped thumbprint into the wet clay just below the rim. Five thousand years later, fragments of these pots – some 300,000 of them – still covered the ground where the potter worked. Dwellings from the Predynastic era rarely survive, but this small, semi-subterranean rectangular house, measuring only 4.0 × 3.5 m (13.1 × 11.4 ft), once composed of posts and mud-coated reeds, can be

Opposite The house of the potter. The charred remnants of the posts that held up the roof still lie just as they fell when burned over 5500 years ago.

Below The appearance of the potter's house can be reconstructed with accuracy from the charred remains.

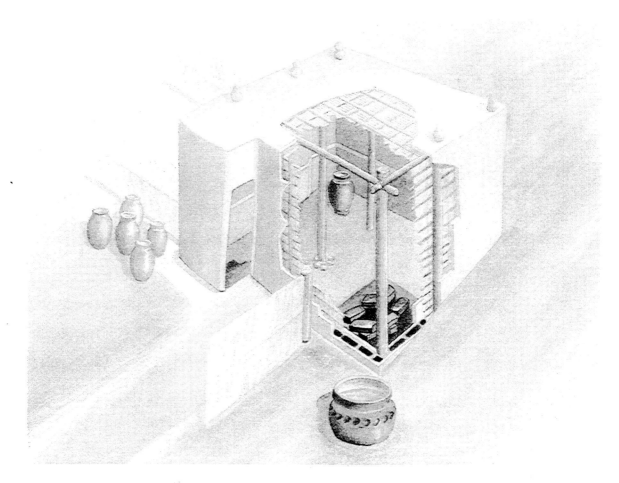

reconstructed due to a fortunate (for us) industrial accident. It would seem that the potter worked a little too close to where he lived, and one day a shift in the wind caused the fire from his pottery kiln, located just over 5 m (16 ft) away, to travel the short distance to the house, setting it alight. The fire reddened and hardened the soil and mud bricks that formed the lower portion of the house and reduced the posts and mats of its walls to charcoal and ash, found by the archaeologists just as they had fallen. Evidence does suggest that the potter wisely rebuilt his house in stone.

On the north side of the town stretched a large industrial zone. Excavations here in 1989 revealed an installation of huge pottery vats for brewing wheat-based beer. This thick and nutritious, only mildly alcoholic, brew was bottled in a range of standardized beer jars, manufactured near by. It is estimated that this brewery, Egypt's earliest, could produce about 1365 litres (300 gallons) of beer a day. At that rate, the brewery could supply a daily ration for over 200 people, and so far only a small fraction of this quarter has been investigated. The centralized collection and redistribution of such resources were ways of saving up against famine and vagaries of the Nile, guarding against chaos, but in good years they could make a king very rich.

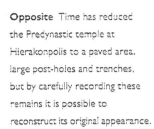

Opposite Time has reduced the Predynastic temple at Hierakonpolis to a paved area, large post-holes and trenches, but by carefully recording these remains it is possible to reconstruct its original appearance.

Above Reconstruction of the Predynastic temple at Hierakonpolis. Huge timber pillars formed the façade of the temple's central shrine, which was made up of colourful woven mats on a timber frame.

Nowhere is the power of the early king more evident than in the centre of this vast town, where in 1985 Egypt's earliest temple began to emerge from beneath the sand. Although post-holes and trenches are all that remain, careful excavation and analysis of the finds leave little doubt about the nature of the complex. In a large oval courtyard stood a solitary pole displaying the image of the god, while at its base, on makeshift platforms, the early kings of

Above Exotic stones were gathered from the far reaches of the desert and transformed into luxury items such as these in the workshops surrounding the temple.

Upper Egypt viewed their bounty and the slaughter made for the falcon god: new-born goats, cattle, crocodiles and even fish, some up to 2 m (6 ft) in length and weighing over 175 kg (386 lb). Around the courtyard, in little workshops, trained craftsmen transformed raw materials gathered from the far reaches of the realm into luxury goods for their princely patrons and their gods; ivory boxes, polished stone jars, jewellery and ceremonial weapons.

The temple's centrepiece was a three-room shrine, its façade made up of four huge timber pillars. From the depth and size of the holes that anchored these pillars we can estimate that they would have been at least 12 m (20 ft) high. To build such a structure, conifers from the forests of Lebanon may have been imported and floated down the Nile. Lavishly appointed with coloured mats for walls, the shrine must have dominated the temple complex and the town of Hierakonpolis as a whole. Destined to become the proto-type for later Egyptian temple architecture, it was a potent symbol of the power of the king and Horus, patron god of Egyptian kingship for the next 3000 years.

Above Until recently the only visible remains at Buto dated to the New Kingdom and later, suggesting to some that the kingdom of Lower Egypt was a myth. Buried below metres of debris, excavations are now finding the remnants of an early culture very different from Upper Egypt.

Buto

The Lower Egyptian counterpart of Hierakonpolis was the city of Buto, and here archaeologists are finding an early community of a very different character. The fact that they are finding anything at all from this period is itself noteworthy.

Today the remains of ancient Buto cover over half a square mile (1 sq. km), but none of the visible ruins, in some places up to 24 m (80 ft) tall, dates to the early periods. As a result, some scholars considered the legend of the 'Souls of Buto' and the existence of a Predynastic kingdom in Lower Egypt to be a myth, and the Delta at that time to have been an uninhabitable swamp. But in 1983 a team from the German Archaeological Institute determined to test this assumption. The main problem was that if early sites existed, they must be buried below several metres of silt brought by the annual Nile flood and the debris of millennia of later occupation.

Geological drill-cores allowed archaeologists to examine the lowest layers below the mound of Buto. Not only did they find the earliest settlement, some 3 m (10 ft) below sea level, but they also discovered that the Delta was not always the well-watered place it is today. In fact, in prehistoric times, parts of the Delta were practically desert. Although various branches of the Nile cut through the Delta plain, it was only in the fifth millennium BC, shortly before the first inhabitants came to Buto, that a rise in the level of the Mediterranean Sea backed up the Nile, causing it to flood its banks. When this occurred, the high tops of sand dunes made a perfect place to escape the inundation, and it is upon a long-buried dune, some 7 m (23.5 ft) below the surface, that the first settlement at Buto was discovered. Well below the water-table, excavation of the early levels could only be done with the help of diesel water pumps. This was difficult and dangerous work: the pumps had to run continuously day and night, since one break in the vacuum suction would allow the water to rush back in minutes.

It is now clear that Buto was the site of continuous Predynastic occupation for over 500 years. The stratified accumulation of debris, mostly hundreds of thousands of pottery sherds, has allowed the expedition director, Dina Faltings, to study the nature of this culture over time. By 'reading' the pottery she can tell that, in striking contrast to the Saharan influences that affected their Upper Egyptian contemporaries, the early Butites looked to the east. Distinctive pots, expertly made on a turning device and decorated with bands of white paint, point to a connection with early cultures in the Negev desert. This interaction was, however, short-lived and the Butites returned to making pottery by their traditional, rather unsophisticated, hand-made methods. They mixed Nile clay with straw or strands of flax, fashioned a lump of clay for the bottom, added some upright slabs and then squeezed it all together to make a pot. After a vessel dried, its surface was rubbed with a pebble, making it more watertight and attractive. But as soon as pottery from Upper Egypt began to appear, its elegance and superior quality were obvious. A makeshift pottery kiln found at Buto in 1995 shows that the Lower Egyptians tried to imitate the Upper Egyptian forms in their own local materials and with their own techniques, but without the specialized knowledge of the Upper Egyptian craftsmen – it wasn't a very successful undertaking.

Less than a hundred years later, these differences had ceased to matter. The indigenous pottery of the Delta had all but vanished and had been replaced with vessels made in Upper Egyptian shapes and in the Upper Egyptian way. The Delta houses were no longer made of bundled papyrus and mats but with mud bricks, as in the south. Moreover, although no cemeteries have yet been located at Buto, the evidence from other Delta sites indicates that even the most traditional of religious beliefs had changed to mirror the Upper Egyptian practice of including valuable grave-goods. This may represent one of the rare cases of archaeological evidence for a political event. It would certainly appear that the 'Two Lands' were not a myth: the Delta and the Valley were originally different lands with different cultures, but by the beginning

Opposite By 'reading' the pottery, Buto expedition director Dina Faltings can trace the development of Predynastic culture in the Delta over time.

of Egyptian history, at about 3100 BC, they had become one. How did this occur? Did Upper Egyptian culture take over the Delta via peaceful commercial contacts, or was it imposed with the help of lethal weapons?

Narmer's Palette

Since its discovery a century ago, the Palette of Narmer has influenced the way we view the unification of Upper and Lower Egypt and the birth of the world's first nation state. Found in a cache of temple offerings at Hierakonpolis in 1898, it was dedicated by King Narmer, possibly the same figure as the legendary King Menes, Egypt's first pharaoh. On one side it depicts Narmer wearing the bulbous 'White Crown' of Upper Egypt about to strike down a prone prisoner in the presence

Above The exquisite slate Palette of King Narmer. On one side Narmer, wearing the White Crown of Upper Egypt, stands with upraised mace about to smite the enemy chief whose name, written in hieroglyphs beside his head, is 'Wash'. The outcome is elucidated by the falcon grasping a symbol of the land and people of the papyrus plant. The meaning is clear: Horus, the patron god of kingship, now controls the Delta. Yet the presence of the foot-washer and sandal-bearer behind the king has suggested to some scholars that the action depicted here is ritual rather than historic.

On the other side Narmer, now wearing the Red Crown of Lower Egypt, marches in procession in the company of high officials to inspect two rows of decapitated foe at a place called the 'door of Horus'. The king's name, written as a catfish (nar) and a chisel (mer), appears before his face and again in the top registers within a panel that represents the gate of the royal palace, or 'great house'. Below, the serpentine necks of the two captive lions frame the dish in which cosmetics were ground, perhaps to dress the divine image of the god. They portray the control and balance of powerful opposing forces vested in the person of the king. Below, as a raging bull, the king tramples town walls and gores its inhabitants to maintain this balance.

Right The 'White Crown' and the 'Red Crown' worn together form the 'Double Crown', the symbol of the king's dominion over the 'Two Lands' of Egypt.

of the falcon god Horus. On the other side, Narmer, wearing the distinctive 'Red Crown' of Lower Egypt, moves in a procession towards two rows of decapitated prisoners. Below, the lions with their serpentine necks intertwined symbolize the unification.

The key element for understanding the palette has always been the crowns. For the first time, one king is shown wearing both the Red and the White Crown. The message seems unambiguous: in about 3100 BC King Narmer of Upper Egypt smites his enemies with the help of his patron god, defeats the Lower Egyptian kingdom and assumes its crown and control – the decisive act of one man.

For the next 3000 years, the same images would reappear. In due course the two crowns would become entwined to form the 'Double Crown', signifying that the pharaoh was the lord of the 'Two Lands', and it would grace the head of every king until the end of Egyptian civilization. The image of the smiting king was inscribed on temple façades throughout Egypt to reinforce his conquest of enemies, both real and metaphoric. However, the

continuous ritual significance of these images has caused some scholars to question the historic interpretation of the Narmer Palette. Could just one object be trusted to tell us so much? New discoveries at Abydos in Upper Egypt are now clarifying this issue.

Abydos

At the mouth of the dramatic canyon at Abydos, which the Egyptians believed to be the entrance to the underworld, lay the tombs of the kings of the first two dynasties. Over 1000 years later, one of these tombs was to be mistaken for that of Osiris, the god of the dead, and for another 1000 years pilgrims would leave millions of little offering vessels in his honour. For this reason, the area is now called in Arabic the 'Omm el Gaab', 'Mother of Pots'.

In 1977 Dr Günter Dreyer of the German Archaeological Institute began reinvestigating the cemeteries at Abydos to fill in blanks left by inadequate and hasty nineteenth-century excavations. Using the exacting standards of modern archaeology, Dreyer has revealed remarkable new finds that are forcing us to re-evaluate the site of Abydos and the early history of Egypt as a whole.

Since the royal tombs were repeatedly pillaged in antiquity and excavated twice in modern times, one wouldn't expect there to be much left to find. Yet new clearance around the tomb of Narmer revealed a tiny ivory label of great importance. On it the name of the king comes alive. As the '*nar*' or catfish (the first element of his name), Narmer smites an enemy out of whose head sprout the papyrus reeds of the Delta marshes. As Dreyer explains:

> 'Such labels served to indicate the date of oil shipments. At that
> time, dates were indicated by the names of years and these names
> were chosen after the most important events of that year. In this
> case, it's a victory of King Narmer over the Delta people and
> obviously it is the same event as depicted on the Narmer Palette.
> From this we may conclude that the Narmer Palette indeed refers
> to an historical event which took place in a certain year.'

Confirmation that Narmer's victory was an actual event rather than a ritual one is welcome new information. However, further discoveries at Abydos show that this event was only one, but perhaps the last, step in a process of unification that had begun at least five generations before Narmer was born.

Excavating in 1988 in an area that had been long neglected to the east of the royal cemetery, Dreyer and his team happened upon a surprisingly

Left Recent excavations have revealed that
even earlier kings were buried at Abydos: kings
of a previously unknown dynasty, Dynasty 0.

Writing

One of the world's most beautiful scripts, the Egypt-ian hieroglyphic writing system consists of hundreds of different signs – pictures of natural and man-made things. However, the script is not a primitive 'picture writing' but a sophisticated system capable of com-municating complex information. The Egyptians had different types of signs: some stand for complete words, usually the object they represent (word signs); but most signify sounds or combinations of

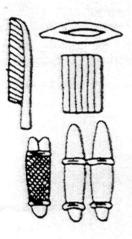

Left Group of five hieroglyphs, including different types of sign. The top three are 'sound signs', writing the word 'irp' meaning 'wine'. Below them are two 'determinatives' representing wine jars, which make the meaning of the word clear.

Above right Clay tablet with early Mesopotamian writing, c.3000 BC.

sounds (sound signs), like our alphabetic characters. For example, the reed leaf stands for the sound 'i', the mouth for the sound 'r', the mat for 'p'. Together these signs phonetically spell 'irp' the word for wine. In addition, a picture of wine jars with no phonetic value could be appended to help determine the sense of the word and prevent any ambiguity. Signs used in this way are called 'determinatives'.

Until recently it was thought that the earliest writing system was invented by the Sumerians in Mesopotamia towards the end of the fourth millen-nium BC and that the idea was borrowed by the Egyptians at the beginning of the First Dynasty (c.3100 BC). However, recent discoveries at Abydos have shown that the Egyptians had an advanced system of writing even earlier than the Mesopotami-ans, some 150 years before Narmer. Remarkably, there is no evidence that this writing developed from a more primitive pictographic stage. Already, at

the very beginning, it incorporated signs for sounds.

Unlike Mesopotamian writing, which can be shown to have gradually evolved through a number of stages, beginning as an accounting system, Egyptian writing appears to have been deliberately invented in a more-or-less finished form, its underlying principles fully in place right from the outset. A parallel for such a process is known from more recent times: in AD 1444 the Korean script (still widely regarded as one of the world's most efficient) was invented by order of the king, who assembled a group of schol-ars for the purpose.

In Egypt this invention corresponds with the birth of the Egyptian state, and its growing administrative and bureaucratic needs. Some of the earliest uses of this writing system were to record the receipt of tax, and denote the origin of commodities and their production date. It was not until much later that sur-viving works of literature and historical records were composed, but the capacity to create such texts was already in place at this early time.

A cursive form of the hieroglyphic script, called hieratic, was soon developed for day-to-day use, when it was normally written in ink on papyrus.

elaborate brick-lined tomb with twelve rooms fitted out as a house for eternity, complete with doors and windows. But this tomb, which they called U-j, was not just a house but a palace. An ivory sceptre, of the kind that formed part of the standard royal regalia of later times, indicates that its owner was clearly the ruler of a previously unknown dynasty, a Dynasty 0, who reigned in about 3250 BC. More importantly, in one of the rooms were 150 small labels

Right Tomb U-j at Abydos was not just a house for eternity but a palace, complete with doors, windows, storerooms and bedchambers, for one of the kings of Dynasty 0, c.3250 BC.

Below Labels from Tomb U-j testify to the existence of a developed writing system over 150 years earlier than previously attested. The label in the lower left-hand corner may spell out the name of the Delta town Bubastis, suggesting that taxes were already being collected from the 'Two Lands' in Dynasty 0.

Below From its inception, the hieroglyphic system used signs for sounds. On the two labels on the left, the tall 'lightning bolt' spells out the word for 'grh' or 'darkness'; the snake is the letter 'dj' which together with the mountain sign below writes 'djw', the word for 'mountain'. On the other three labels, the word for mountain appears again, but this time with a crested ibis, which spells 'akh', meaning 'lightness'. Together these inscriptions can be read as the 'mountains of darkness' and the 'mountains of light', or the western and eastern mountains.

of ivory or bone, many of which appear to have been attached to bolts of linen. Carved on some of them are numbers indicating amounts or size, but on others are recognizable and readable hieroglyphic signs which spell out phonetically the names of places from which these goods originated. Small and laconic as they are, these labels testify to the existence of a developed writing system over a hundred years earlier than we ever expected.

What is equally surprising about the labels from this tomb is that some of the named places are in the Delta, suggesting that taxes and tribute were already being collected from Lower Egypt. In addition, hundreds of wine jars imported from Canaan, stacked three deep in one of the tomb's stone rooms, indicate that a well-established trade, passing through Lower Egyptian territory, was now firmly in the hands of this Upper Egyptian king. But who was this ruler, perhaps one of the earliest to rule the two lands of Egypt? Dreyer suggests that his name be read as Scorpion, as many pottery vessels had this name written in ink on them. But there were other names as well, simple names written with an animal sign: sea-shell, dog, lion and elephant – perhaps the members of a royal dynasty that even the Egyptians were later to forget or only vaguely remember as demigods. Further research may yet make them mortals.

Memphis

To crown the achievement of a unified nation, the early kings moved their capital to a suitable place from which to administer the Two Lands. They chose a spot at the southern apex of the Delta so strategic that it remained the administrative centre of the country until Roman times. Located a little to the south and across the river from modern Cairo, the Greeks called it Memphis. To the Egyptians it was appropriately 'The Balance of the Two Lands'. It was also called 'The White Walls', probably in reference to the gleaming walls surrounding its most important landmark, the king's palace. It is possible that the founding of this magnificent city marked the beginning of recorded factual history about Egypt's early kings, but the proof of this depends on finding the actual remains of the first city at Memphis. These, however, have remained elusive until recently.

Spreading around the modern village of Mit Rahina, the visible mounds and later ruins of Memphis have always been thought to cover the spot of its first foundation. When an expedition of the Egypt Exploration Society, now headed by David Jeffreys, began to survey the massive ruin fields in 1982, the results were surprising. They found that, unlike sites such as Buto, for example, Memphis was not a giant layer cake with superimposed levels of continuous occupation stretching back in time. Instead, the city appeared to be constantly, if sometimes only gradually, shifting. The reason for this was the Nile. In ancient times, the course of the river was not set, and after a high flood the Nile could retreat to a different channel. Over time it moved

Opposite David Jeffreys searches for the first city of Memphis using manual drill cores.

Overleaf The visible remains of Memphis near the modern village of Mit Rahina do not mark the location of the original city.

further and further to the east, and with it moved the city. When the expedition located the New Kingdom city in one place and the town of the Middle Kingdom further to the west, it became clear that the evidence for the first 1000 years of the city's life had to lie even closer to the desert's edge, but where?

Considering the northern location of the numerous First Dynasty cemeteries in the Memphite region, David Jeffreys realized that the first city had to be somewhere close by. As the first to use the Saqqara plateau, site of the ancient necropolis for Memphis, the early officials had an unlimited choice of places to build their impressive tombs, and Jeffreys assumed they would have chosen locations close to home. Geological corings are beginning to verify this assumption. Remnants of the early town have been found some 2 miles (3 km) northwest of the Memphis ruin fields and close to the western escarpment. Unfortunately they are buried several metres down and well below the water-table, so it may be many years before excavations can expose the marvels of the first national capital. Yet dozens of laboriously hand-turned corings do provide a picture of the deposits buried beneath the modern topsoil and have revealed another surprising twist to the story of early Memphis.

Alternating bands of silt and sand in the cores testify to a series of climatic changes when the Nile floods were alternately low or high. Too high and the town was flooded, houses of unfired mud brick collapsed and cattle drowned; too low and the sands from the west blew in and carpeted the valley floor with a taste of the desert. These were the forces of chaos at work, and it was the king's job to control them by providing the appropriate disaster relief, either by feeding the famine-stricken or marshalling the manpower

Below Over time – from its first foundation to modern times – the city of Memphis shifted its position as the river altered its course.

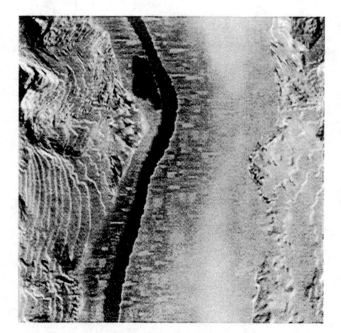
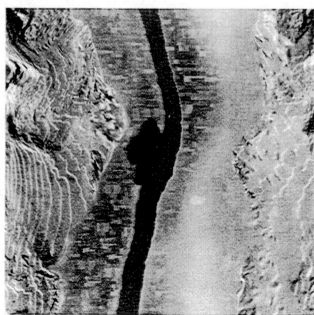

for rebuilding. But above all, it was his responsibility to propitiate the gods who caused such chaos and to redress the all-important cosmic balance.

The Famine Stela inscribed on Sehel Island at the First Cataract of the Nile describes such an event. In it, King Djoser, a Third Dynasty king who is famous as the builder of the Step Pyramid, gives his thanks in the form of rich gifts to the gods of the cataract region for ending the distress caused by seven years of low Nile floods. Although carved over 2000 years after Djoser's reign to bolster the claim of the priesthood to certain revenues, in light of the new evidence from Memphis, it may actually be based on historic fact.

Above The Famine Stela at Sehel Island near the First Cataract of the Nile describes a seven-year famine during the time of King Djoser. Ptolemaic Period.

In this case and others, the king was apparently able to handle the crisis. Yet the geological cores reveal that at the end of the Old Kingdom, approximately 1000 years after its founding, early Memphis was engulfed by a huge sand-dune, evidence of a sustained period of low Nile floods and searing heat. This was just one of the many disasters that befell all of Egypt at this

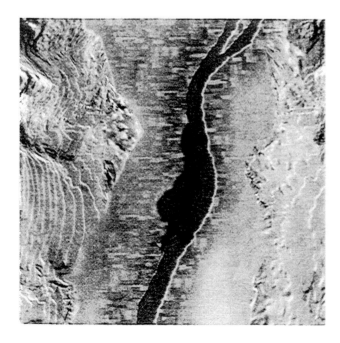

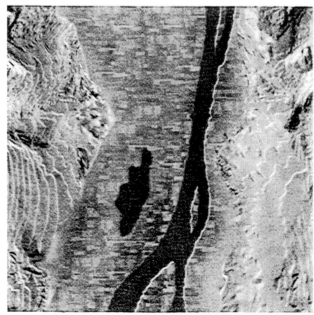

Above The 'Dam of the Pagans' at Helwan was the first great attempt at flood control in history, but unfortunately it was destroyed by water before it was completed. Fourth Dynasty, c.2600 BC.

time, disrupting the unity of the land and bringing the country to its knees. Sometimes, despite the efforts of the kings, chaos won.

The Helwan Dam

Pharaohs were expected not simply to react to the powers of chaos when disaster struck, but to be proactive as well. To protect Memphis from the Nile, Herodotus relates that its founder, the legendary King Menes, built dikes and dams. The truth of this remains to be ascertained, but near Helwan, about 20 miles (32 km) south of Cairo, the ruins of the world's oldest dam testify to the civil engineering abilities of the pharaohs at the very dawn of the Pyramid Age.

Seth, the chief god of chaos and confusion, was appropriately also the god of the desert and the thunderstorm, for within hours the occasional thunderstorm in the desert can produce a flash-flood of terrifying and destructive intensity. It was to control such flash-floods that the dam was constructed. Called 'Sadd el-Kafara', or 'Dam of the Pagans', it was discovered in 1885 about 7.5 miles (12 km) into the desert. Yet it had to wait almost a hundred years before engineers and archaeologists uncovered its full story.

A remarkable engineering feat, the dam consists of three parts: a loose filling of rubble, encased between two roughly built walls, which were each faced with dressed blocks of stone. Over 98 m (321 ft) wide at the bottom and 56 m (184 ft) across at the top, the dam was designed to be 14 m (46 ft) high and 110 m (361 ft) long. Günter Dreyer of the German Archaeological Institute, working with hydraulic engineers from the Technical University of Braunschweig, estimates that it took about 500 workmen to build it. These men were housed in barracks, which Dreyer helped to uncover on the northern side of the dam in 1982. A good 75 per cent of the workforce must have been engaged in hauling the rubble and stone – some 80,000 cubic metres (104,640 cubic yards) of it – probably on a seasonal basis during the three months of the Nile flood. The remainder – supervisors, stone cutters and food providers – may have worked on a year-round basis for up to ten or twelve years.

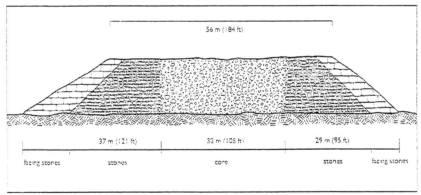

56 m (184 ft)				
37 m (121 ft)		32 m (105 ft)		29 m (95 ft)
facing stones	stones	core	stones	facing stones

Above right The dam consisted of three parts: a filling of rubble in the centre, held in place by rough masonry walls, which were then covered with dressed stone blocks, still visible today.
(After Gaarbrecht and Bertram)

By modern calculations, the dam was over-designed, but nevertheless based on sound hydrological knowledge. It would have served its purpose had it been completed. Unfortunately, with 70 per cent of the construction complete, the first great dam in history was destroyed by the chaos it was built to control, when a massive flash-flood swept the unfinished central section away. The intensity of this flood must have had catastrophic consequences downstream in the quarrying and loading docks which the dam was meant to protect. Perhaps with these installations now in ruins, there was little point in continuing the construction of the dam and all work was abandoned. Tragically, it was just a matter of three years on either side. Had it rained three years earlier, before the construction had reached the *wadi* (dry valley) bed, little of the work would have been washed away. Had it rained

Below The scene on this palette is an early allegory on chaos and order. The animals, in a riot of forms, conflicts and postures, are animated by the very picture of order turned upside-down: a flute-playing jackal in the bottom-left corner. Yet, all is contained and controlled by the perfect harmony of fierce hunting dogs which frame the scene. The Two Dog Palette, from Hierakonpolis. c.3200 BC.

three years later, the flood would certainly have been contained by the completed edifice. In the end, ten years' labour was for nought, and it would be many more years before the Egyptians tried something like this again.

Weni

The ability of the pharaoh to command a large workforce to fight chaos was not limited to the occasionally unsuccessful battles to control the forces of nature. Chaos in a human form also threatened the delicate balance that it was the pharaoh's role to maintain. Although there are numerous visual tributes to the victories won by the kings of the early dynasties over a human foe, it is not until later that texts are preserved which give a more detailed picture of the king's power.

In about 2280 BC a senior court official named Weni recorded the notable events of his life on a monolithic slab of limestone set into his tomb at Abydos. Weni relates how his pharaoh, King Pepi I of the Sixth Dynasty, dealt with the marauding powers of chaos.

'When his majesty took action against the Sand Dwellers of the east, his majesty made an army of many tens of thousands from all over Upper Egypt...There were counts, seal-bearers, chieftains and mayors, chief priests and desert scouts...I was the one who commanded them all...This army returned in safety. It had ravaged the Sand Dwellers' land, it had sacked its strongholds, it had thrown fire into all of its mansions...His majesty sent me to lead this army five times, to attack the land of the Sand Dwellers as often as they rebelled... His majesty praised me for it more than anything.'

While the protection of his citizenry and his borders were of foremost concern to the pharaoh, it would appear that the chief benefits of these bellicose campaigns related to the king's economic interests. The Egyptians professed a horror for the chaos of the desert, the land of Seth, and a strong distaste for those lands and peoples beyond the borders of their own well-ordered world. Yet that never stopped them from going to these places, for they had many things to offer. The desert to the east of the Nile Valley, in particular, had great mineral wealth: not only gold and copper, but also fine stones and semi-precious gems with which to feed the Egyptians' ever-growing appetite for beautiful things. Exploited already in Predynastic times, a new discovery in the Eastern Desert shows that, by the beginning of the First Dynasty, the desert's bounty may well have been under the king's control.

Wadi Abu Had

About 30 miles (50 km) west of the Red Sea coast is the Wadi Abu Had. It is a wide valley bisected by white limestone ridges and occasional green groves of acacia trees, bounded by majestic red granite peaks which contrast with the black basalt hills. Overwhelmed by this colour combination of spectacular beauty, the casual traveller in this wilderness wouldn't cast a glance at the low ridge near the *wadi* centre. Here it was, however, that during an intensive survey in 1993, Ann Bomann of the American School of Oriental Research

Below At Wadi Abu Had, in the wilderness of the Eastern Desert, excavations show that rock crystal, amethyst and malachite were collected, processed and prepared for shipment to the Nile Valley.

spotted a series of interlocking semicircular rough-stone walls in a depression cut out of the soft limestone. Two seasons of excavation showed that inside these walls and beneath their once tent-like roofs, desert resources were collected and processed. Cobbles of basalt were heated and crushed to give up their veins of malachite, a green powder of copper, used as eye make-up. Rock crystal was gathered and flaked. Rough amethysts, mined in nearby granite cliffs, were collected, and the precious purple crystals were refined. While a small band of workmen here prepared their harvest for shipment to the Nile Valley, the marks on the pottery vessels found within the complex indicate that supplies from centralized government storehouses kept them alive.

This collection station was ideally situated at the confluence of three passes through the desert within easy access of transport caravans bringing back any of a number of other treasures. It was one in a network of trading depots, and possibly even colonial administrative centres, which stretched across northern Sinai and half way up the Levantine coast. But by the end of the First Dynasty, all were abandoned for reasons unknown. It would be another millennium before the Egyptians could sustain such a broad imperial vision. In the meantime, it would seem that it was more efficient to send out expeditions, sometimes on a large scale, to get what they wanted by whatever means necessary.

Harkhuf

To lead an expedition beyond the boundaries of the ordered world required bravery and skill. Such men were highly regarded and well compensated. Among the most famous of them was a man named Harkhuf. He was based at Elephantine, at the First Cataract of the Nile – the perfect place from which to launch, at his majesty's bidding, expeditions to the south to bring back for him the exotic treasures of Africa. In his tomb in the cliffs at Qubbet el-Hawa overlooking his town, Harkhuf relates the notable events of his four expeditions into Nubia, 'to bring the produce of all foreign lands to his lord', by casting the 'dread of Horus into the foreign lands'. He boasts of the donkey-loads of incense, ebony, oils, panther skins, elephant tusks and throwsticks he procured in the south lands, but he is most proud of a far more exotic acquisition: a dancing pygmy.

When apprised of the news, King Pepi II himself (c.2278–2184 BC), the last king of the Sixth Dynasty, who was a boy of no more than nine years of age at the time, was compelled to write to Harkhuf in his own hand. A royal

Left The brave men who led expeditions into Africa to bring back its treasures for their king were buried in cliffs overlooking the First Cataract of the Nile.

letter was an honour so rarely bestowed that Harkhuf placed a verbatim copy of its text, grammatical mistakes and all, on the façade of his tomb. In it the boy king's anticipation is palpable:

> 'Come north to the palace at once! Hurry and bring with you this pygmy whom you brought from the land of the horizon dwellers who does the dances of the gods. When he goes with you into the ship, place worthy men around him on deck, lest he fall into the water! When he sleeps, surround him with worthy men in his tent. Inspect him ten times a night. My majesty wishes to see this pygmy more than the gifts of the mine-lands. Orders have been given to the town mayors and overseers of priests that supplies are to be furnished for you from every storage depot and every temple.'

In theory, if not in reality, the king owned everything and it was his to command at his will. In return he maintained the balance of the universe with justice and piety, and did battle with the undefeatable powers of chaos, be they natural phenomena, social upheaval or supernatural forces. With the skills perhaps forged by distant ancestors facing a hostile environment in the desert and honed over the centuries along the banks of an ever-changing Nile, the pharaohs had learned how to raise an army, organize a workforce or prepare a trading expedition. They knew how to gather taxes in times of plenty and distribute supplies in times of need. The longevity of Egyptian civilization is testimony to their abilities.

But each king met one final challenge, one final battle with chaos – the battle for eternal life. For although the king was a god, he was also a man, and he was going to die. The afterlife waited, but it was in no way guaranteed, and the way there was fraught with danger. The chaotic elements from which re-creation could be forged had to be confronted, negotiated and controlled for the king's resurrection to be complete.

By 2700 BC the stage was set for the maximum test of all the king's skills for this ultimate challenge. Men began hauling huge stone blocks to the desert's edge. A new type of monument arose to keep chaos at bay. The age of the pyramids had begun.

RESURRECT

ION
MACHINE

It was the hope of every Egyptian to be reborn after death, to attain an afterlife with the sun-god Ra and be resurrected with each sunrise, and to join with Osiris in the cyclical regeneration of nature and plant life with the receding of the annual Nile flood. These are not opposing beliefs, but a complementary interweaving of the varying cycles of creation with which the Egyptians linked their own eternal rebirth. However, neither the annual rise of the life-giving waters of the Nile nor the re-emergence of the sun each morning was guaranteed. Eternal night and the cessation of plant life were constant threats which had to be averted so that creation could begin again. In the same way, formidable obstacles had to be overcome for resurrection to be achieved.

The journey to the next world was perilous: demons waited to sidetrack the unprepared, judgements were made. Most people had to depend on their family to provide the proper equipment and chant the appropriate spells to help them attain the afterlife. But the king could call upon the resources of the entire country in his bid for immortality. The greatest manifestation of this is seen in the pyramids of the Giza Plateau.

The three pyramids at Giza are the most visited attraction in Egypt, if not the world. The Great Pyramid of the Fourth Dynasty king Khufu, the ultimate 'resurrection machine', is the largest

Left The pyramids at Giza. The middle pyramid built by Khafra is actually half a metre (2 ft) smaller than its neighbour (to the right), the Great Pyramid of Khufu, but built on higher ground it appears to dominate the plateau.

Above left An enormous support system was needed to create and maintain the pyramids, including ancillary staff to produce food, pottery and building supplies. Servant statues from Giza. Old Kingdom, c.2500 BC.

pyramid ever built. It stands with its neighbours, the pyramids of Khafra and Menkaura, as the last remaining of the Seven Wonders of the Ancient World. The immense size of these pyramids invites comparison with the most ambitious human projects of any age, and they have never ceased to fire people's imagination. The first surviving description of them is by the fifth-century BC Greek traveller Herodotus, who also began the tradition of fantastic stories which surround them still today. Herodotus is called the father of history, but the emphasis was on the story – after all he had an audience to entertain, both as readers and on the lecture circuit.

In one tale of whimsy, Herodotus relates that King Cheops, the Greek name for Khufu, was so evil a man that for lack of money to build his massive pyramid he confined his own daughter to a chamber, where she had to receive clients and exact payment for her services. She, in addition, demanded that each man give her one stone so that she could build her own pyramid, this being identified as one of the three queen's pyramids in front of the Great Pyramid today. Herodotus also reports that his guides said that both Cheops and Chephren (Khafra) shut the temples to divert payment to their tombs, placing the land in such great misery that in his day their memory was hated. Be that as it may, power has never before or since been so massively concentrated or so physically expressed as in the pyramids of these Fourth Dynasty kings.

Both Herodotus and Egyptian texts explicitly state that pyramids served as tombs, and the archaeological evidence confirms this beyond doubt. Nevertheless, from the nineteenth century onwards, bizarre theories about their function have proliferated, insisting that the Great Pyramid in particular served a hidden, more exalted purpose. Interpreted variously as an astronomical observatory, sundial, the embodiment of secret knowledge about the past and the future, the Great Pyramid has been held to be the perfect structure and the product of divine inspiration. Such 'pyramidiocy' has sometimes been promoted for political reasons. For example, calculations (not necessarily accurate) revealed that the basic unit of measure used in the construction of the Great Pyramid was remarkably similar to the English inch. As the perfect unit in a divine creation, to abandon the inch for the metric system, as Parliament was considering in 1874, would be a blasphemous and pagan act; and indeed, partly for this reason among others, the move was rejected.

In more recent times, pyramidiocy has resurfaced in various updated forms. As our horizons have broadened, it is not just secret biblical knowledge that has been discerned encrypted in the form and dimensions of the Great Pyramid, but extra-terrestrial intelligence as well. Yet even the most bizarre theories concerning master races and alien origins for these supreme Egyptian creations in their way pay tribute to the Fourth Dynasty rulers, simply by expressing incredulity that they could organize and complete so colossal a task.

The Pyramid Builders of the Old Kingdom

Third Dynasty

Djoser	c. 2686–2667 BC
Sekhemkhet	2648–2640
Khaba	2640–2637
Huni	2637–2613

Fourth Dynasty

Snefru	c. 2613–2589 BC
Khufu	2589–2566
Djedfra	2566–2558
Khafra	2558–2532
Menkaura	2532–2503

Fifth Dynasty

Userkaf	c.2494–2487 BC
Sahura	2487–2475
Neferirkara	2475–2455
Shepseskara	2455–2448
Raneferef	2448–2445
Niuserra	2445–2421
Menkauhor	2421–2414
Djedkara-Isesi	2414–2375
Unas	2375–2345

Sixth Dynasty

Teti	c.2345–2323 BC
Pepi I	2321–2287
Merenra	2287–2278
Pepi II	2278–2184

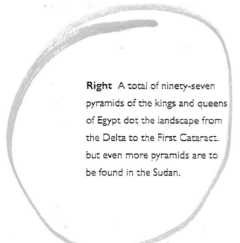

Right A total of ninety-seven pyramids of the kings and queens of Egypt dot the landscape from the Delta to the First Cataract. but even more pyramids are to be found in the Sudan.

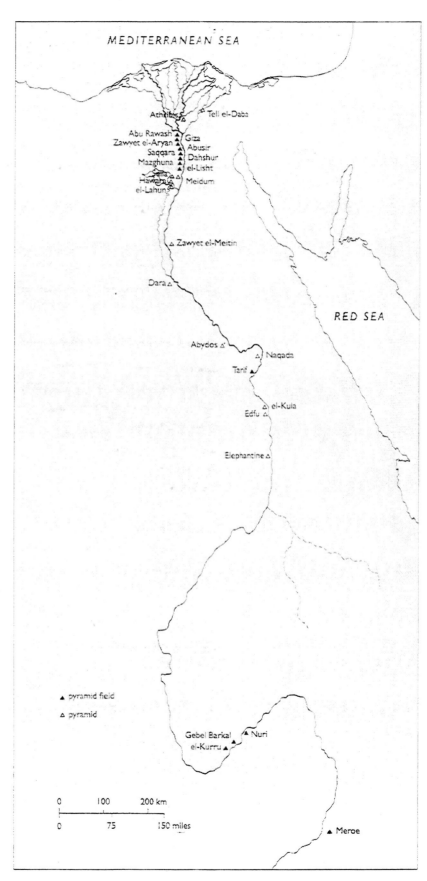

Pyramids, however, are not restricted to Giza, nor are they phenomena only of the Fourth Dynasty. The origins of the pyramid begin well before the 'Pyramid Age' of the Old Kingdom and end long after. For over one thousand years Egyptian kings built tombs for themselves and their queens in the form of pyramids. There are in fact over ninety 'royal' pyramids in Egypt, dotting the landscape from the apex of the Delta to the First Cataract of the Nile. Remarkably, at least twice as many again are to be found further south, in modern day Sudan, the ancient land of Kush. Some 2000 years after the first pyramid was constructed, the native Sudanese kings of Kush returned to the pyramid form for their tombs, ushering in yet another millennium of pyramid building. Revived and reinterpreted in a style strictly their own, the Kushite kings kept the pyramid alive long after the culture which invented it was moribund. In fact, it was not until the introduction of Christianity and a distinctly different view of how the afterlife might be attained that the venerable art of pyramid building on the African continent finally came to an end.

The Resurrection Machine

To understand the origins of the pyramids one must go back to the very beginning, the beginning of the world as the Egyptians saw it. For at this time there was only a watery void called Nun, which contained the essence of all creation. Out of this chaotic yet creative soup arose a mound, just as the mounds of fertile silt teeming with life emerged as the waters of the annual Nile flood receded. On that mound of creation appeared the sun god Ra–Atum, embodiment of life and goodness, the source of energy, light and warmth. From him the rest of creation issued forth as he rose in the sky, only to plunge back into the chaotic void with every sunset to be re-created again. For the Egyptians, creation unfolded not once, but continuously. By linking up with this cosmic cycle, they too could emerge reborn.

The pyramid was essentially this mound of creation, a cocoon in which the king underwent the transformation or recreation into an eternal transfigured spirit called an *akh*. Journeying to the sky, he was united with the gods and resurrected each morning.

But the pyramid itself was only one part of the resurrection machine. Like all gods, the king was in permanent need of the sustenance and offerings which were provided to him on earth. Thus the pyramid alone was not enough to ensure a good afterlife. In time elaborate complexes developed which incorporated the pyramid and offering places, ranging from small chapels to a vast series of interconnected temples and estates, to service the needs of the deceased pharaoh on earth. No pyramid or pyramid complex is exactly like another. Their continuous development can be understood not only in terms of technological innovation and evolving religious beliefs, but also of the desire to ensure the absolute and eternal power of the resurrection machine to do its job.

The Prehistory of Pyramids

By the beginning of the First Dynasty, if not earlier, the mound of sand and rubble heaped on top of a grave, perhaps initially as a marker, had become associated with the primordial mound of creation.

Out in the desert at Abydos, the first kings of Egypt were buried in deep brick-lined tombs topped with square or rectangular mounds of sand which Egyptologists call 'mastabas', due to their resemblance to the benches that once stood in front of modern Egyptian village homes. So important was the mound over these royal tombs, that by the middle of the First Dynasty, the

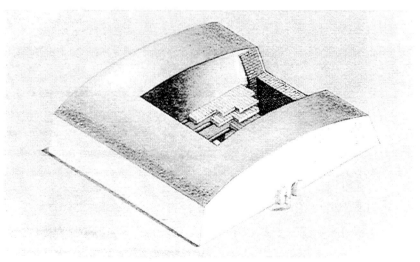

Above In the First Dynasty tomb of King Den (c.2950 BC) the remnants of the retaining walls that once held the mounds are still visible.

Right The early kings constructed two mounds over their deep, brick-lined tombs: one directly above the tomb itself, but still below ground; and one above ground to cover and protect the one below.

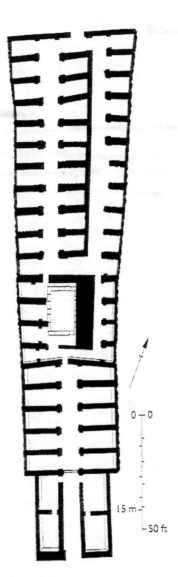

Left A plan of Khasekhemwy's tomb made after its first excavation almost a hundred years ago.

builders constructed two of them. One was placed underground, supported by a retaining wall, directly over the stout roofing beams that covered the increasingly elaborate tombs. The second mastaba, encased in a mud-brick wall, was placed above ground, directly over the first. Clearly the early kings had come to see that various chaotic forces, such as rain or flash-floods and wind storms, could destroy the burial mound and interrupt resurrection much in the same way they feared chaos could interfere with the actual cycle of cosmic creation. The upper mastaba was designed to protect the lower mastaba and doubled the chances of survival in this world and the next. This

reinforcement and multiplication of the mound later played a part in the
genesis of the pyramid.

With each generation the royal tombs became more elaborate, containing
a huge number of sumptuous offerings and surrounded by the graves of
wives, household retainers, servants and even pets. The largest and the last
royal tomb to be built at Abydos is that of King Khasekhemwy, the last king
of the Second Dynasty who ruled Egypt to about 2686 BC. Since 1995 Dr
Günter Dreyer of the German Archaeological Institute has been re-investi-
gating his tomb, clearing away the sand that has covered it since its initial

Above Khasekhemwy's funerary enclosure is today called 'Shunet es-Zebib', the 'Storehouse of the Flies', a name derived from the local legend that it was one of the granaries that Joseph used for storing the harvest against the seven lean years, as related in the Bible. The decoration of recesses or niches on the exterior walls of Khasekhemwy's palace of eternity imitates the appearance of the palace he used in life.

excavation a century ago. Completely unlike the tombs of his predecessors, Khasekhemwy's tomb is trapezoidal in shape and impressively large. In a trench dug deep in the sand, it was constructed of mud brick and measures almost 69 m (230 ft) in length, varying in width between 17.6 m (56 ft) and 10.4 m (33 ft).

After two seasons, Dreyer has succeeded in clearing again the first part of the tomb, which was made up of thirty-three storage rooms for offerings and funerary equipment laid out in three rows. His careful study of the architectural remains has revealed a fascinating story of structural collapse which protected valuable burial equipment from the robbers who burrowed through the walls to get at it; further large-scale pillaging was followed by pious restoration in the Middle Kingdom, many centuries after the tomb was built. However, Dreyer has yet to reach the really interesting part of the tomb, the burial chamber – a room built entirely of dressed stone blocks. At the time of its initial discovery, this chamber was the earliest stone construction then known, and, although earlier examples of stone masonry have since been found, Khasekhemwy's remains the finest of its age. New research suggests it is but a mere hint of what he was capable.

While such tombs were the private chambers of the king for eternity, at the edge of the desert about half a mile (1 km) away each king built for himself an eternal palace of state: a place where the official and ritual business of a king could be undertaken for eternity, and where eternal tribute and nourishment would be supplied.

No doubt based on the actual palace that the king used during his lifetime, many of these massive mud-brick enclosures were decorated on their outer surface with a series of niches or recesses to create a panelled effect. Professor David O'Connor of the Institute of Fine Arts, New York, has been studying these enclosures for many years. Although most have been reduced to a scant few courses of brickwork, traces of a whitewash coating are still preserved. The result must have been dazzling, as an intricate pattern of light and shadow was reflected across these brilliant white-panelled walls over the course of the day. It is not surprising therefore, that this architectural style was to have a lasting influence in Egypt. Before the invention of the cartouche to enclose a king's name (see page 16), the image of the niched façade of the royal palace was used. The king's name was inscribed as if on the lintel over an elaborately panelled gateway in a device called a *serekh*. Subsequently, the whole design of panels, recesses and doors became the fixed scheme for the carved stone sarcophagi of royalty and the élite alike throughout the Old Kingdom and later. In effect, the sarcophagus became each person's individual palace of eternity.

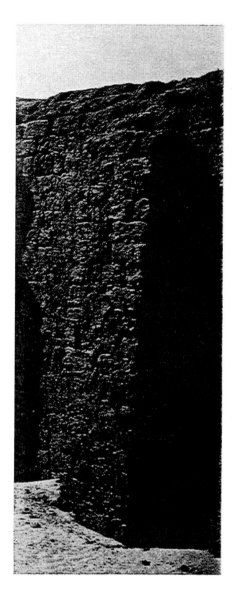

Khasekhemwy's is the only one of these palaces of eternity at Abydos still clearly visible. In fact, it is hard to miss. Still standing in places to its full original height of 11 m (36 ft), with walls 5.5 m (18 ft) thick, it is one of the oldest standing mud-brick structures in the world. It measures 122 m (400 ft) in length and 65 m (213 ft) wide and is surrounded by a low curtain wall. Unfortunately, little remains within the structure to help determine how it might have functioned, since buildings of temporary and perishable materials have vanished. However, clearance of a portion of the vast enclosed space in 1988 by O'Connor and his team uncovered a large mound of sand and gravel covered with a brick skin near the centre of the structure. Its

Right King Khasekhemwy wears the White Crown of Upper Egypt on one of the most ancient datable statues in the world and possibly the earliest representation in the round of a known historical personage. One of a pair of statues from Hierakonpolis. Limestone. c.2690 BC.

Above On the funerary stela of the First Dynasty king Wadje, the niched façade of his palace is reproduced as the device called a *serekh* to hold his name. c.2980 BC.

significance is not entirely clear. Perhaps it formed another 'mound of creation', signifying the presence of the king's resurrected spirit; and as such it is another step toward the birth of the pyramid.

This king's ability to marshal a workforce to construct such a massive tomb and vast mortuary palace is as impressive as the structures themselves. Millions of mud bricks were involved, some of which had to be hauled over a mile into the desert to be put in place. But Khasekhemwy didn't just build one of these palatial enclosures, he built another at Hierakonpolis. Only one-third the size of the enclosure at Abydos, it was nevertheless no mean feat, and it too still stands to its original height, a testament to its builders' construction skills. The real story of the pyramids begins here, in terms of the organizational aspect alone.

Khasekhemwy, although little known, was the first major builder among the pharaohs, but he didn't stop with the building of tombs. The accomplished relief carving on the hard stone architectural features that embellished both his enclosure and the temple of Horus at Hierakonpolis, as well as the two stone statues of himself that he dedicated there, anticipates the formal style and poses of Egyptian art which were to follow. Khasekhemwy

Above Khasekhemwy's enclosure at Hierakonpolis, the oldest standing brick building in Egypt.

Right A graffito left by an ancient Egyptian tourist who visited the Step Pyramid one thousand years after it was built.

had taken Egypt to the cusp of the Old Kingdom, the first great flowering of Egyptian civilization. Massive constructions of mud brick and refined carving of hard stone were well within his control. But it seems that Khasekhemwy may have had even greater aspirations, further north, at Saqqara.

The Step Pyramid

Saqqara was the site of the necropolis of ancient Memphis. It is dominated by the Step Pyramid of King Djoser, the first of Egypt's pyramids and one of the most remarkable architectural achievements of the ancient Egyptians. Constructed entirely of stone, the pyramid is surrounded by a complex in which the originally wooden and mud-brick structures of the palace were faithfully rendered in stone. This was truly a palace of eternity, built for the first time in the world entirely of imperishable stone. The careful restoration of the complex over the past fifty years by the French architect Jean-Phillipe Lauer allows one to experience some of the awe felt by ancient Egyptian tourists who visited the site over one thousand years after it was built. Ancient graffiti record their impressions and admiration:

> 'The Scribe Ahmose came to see the Temple of Djoser. He found it as though heaven were inside it, Ra rising within, heaven raining myrrh and incense dripping upon it.'

It is, in fact, from these graffiti that the owner of the pyramid, a mysterious King Netjerikhet, could be equated with King Djoser, known from the historical king-lists.

Captured in the permanence of stone was a moment in time for the king's eternal use. Not just any moment, but the festival of rejuvenation the king would have celebrated in his lifetime in his thirtieth year on the throne. Assembled are the shrines of the gods from all over the country to welcome

Above Imhotep, King Djoser's architect, was later deified as a god of architecture and medicine. Bronze statuette. Late Period, after 600 BC.

Opposite The Step Pyramid and its associated structures form the first monumental funerary complex built entirely of stone.

him and acclaim him after completing a ritual test of his virility. Offices of state and an extensive temple fill the north end of the complex, and all are surrounded by a niched stone wall.

The magnificence of this complex earned Djoser immortality, but greater fame went to its architect, a man of learning named Imhotep, who was credited with the invention of working in hewn stone, major works of medicine and literature, and although a common man was later deified as a saint.

The Step Pyramid complex represents a dramatic increase in technical progress and artistic accomplishment – advances made in a remarkably short period of time. Even today, this quantum leap from the use of stone for details such as the stone-lined chamber in the tomb of Khasekhemwy to the raising of huge monuments built exclusively of this material has been attributed to Imhotep's vision and aptitude. However, new work suggests that the way, in fact, had already been paved.

Gisr el Mudir

To the west of the Step Pyramid, the desert looks barren, but emerging from the drift sand here and there are the stone masonry walls of rectangular enclosures. The largest of these mysterious monuments is called the Gisr el Mudir, or 'enclosure of the boss'. First noted in the nineteenth century, the full extent of this enclosure was not appreciated until aerial photographs in the 1920s revealed it to be enormous, and it has intrigued Egyptologists ever since. Measuring about 350 × 650 m (1150 × 2130 ft), it is almost twice the size of the Step Pyramid enclosure. However, the excavation of such an immense complex, its walls stretching to the horizon, is a task only slightly less daunting than building it in the first place, and as a result, its age, purpose and accurate dimensions long remained a subject of speculation. Only recently have cost-efficient means for answering these questions been developed.

Ian Mathieson of the National Museums of Scotland is using some of this new technology. With an electric resistivity meter, which measures the resistance of buried features to an electrical current passed through the ground, he is mapping the subsurface topography of the Gisr el Mudir without ever shifting a shovel of sand. In this way, excavations can be directed to specific parts of this vast area which show special promise for answering the many outstanding questions. After particularly high readings, selected areas along the face of the walls were chosen for further investigation. Here Mathieson uncovered fifteen courses of limestone masonry, a stone wall still about 4.5 m (15 ft) high. The intended height must have been much greater, as the walls are an astounding 15 m (49 ft) thick, composed of rubble fill with a masonry skin for the majority of their length, but solidly built of roughly dressed stone at the corners. According to Mathieson, the enclosure must have been the largest stone construction that anyone could have built at that time in history. It is especially impressive, as pottery recovered from these excavations

Above An electric resistivity meter is used by Ian Mathieson and his team to detect features buried beneath the vast area of the Gisr el Mudir.

indicates that the enclosure's construction predates King Djoser by some years. It, not the Step Pyramid complex, may in fact be the oldest building in stone, although it was apparently never completed. Exactly who was responsible for it still remains unknown, but it is hard to imagine anyone other than the great builder King Khasekhemwy who, at the end of his reign, may have made an even bigger and better bid for immortality, this time in stone.

Right Excavations along the west and north walls of the Gisr el Mudir revealed the incredible size of its stone walls.

Opposite The enormous rectangle to the west of the Step Pyramid has puzzled Egyptologists ever since it size was made clear from aerial photographs. It is called the Gisr el Mudir, 'the enclosure of the boss'.

The probability that Khasekhemwy was responsible for the Gisr el Mudir is strengthened by a recent discovery from his tomb at Abydos. Although Khasekhemwy is known to have been the last king of the Second Dynasty, the identity of his successor long remained unclear. Working at the north entrance to the tomb, however, Günter Dreyer came upon an area that had never been cleared before. Here, around the door, he found several seal impressions of King Djoser. Clearly, Djoser must have buried Khasekhemwy, closing his tomb and placing upon it his royal seal. Burying one's predecessor was the duty of every king, and for the first time we now know that King Djoser must have been the immediate successor to Khasekhemwy and may even have been his step-son. What this new discovery shows is that, probably not for the first time and certainly not for the last, a ruler has been given credit for advances made by his predecessor.

The Step Pyramid and its Descendants

According to Dreyer, this succession is important for understanding the development of the Step Pyramid. With the ability to quarry, transport and lay large quantities of stone already developed, Imhotep's true innovation appears to have been combining the two elements of the tomb and the funerary palace in a new way. As Dreyer explains:

> 'When Djoser built his tomb he decided to bring the two elements, tomb and large enclosure, together but what happened? He built his tomb shaft, the chamber and the mound above, the initial mastaba over that and then the enclosure wall was built around it. But now the important mound, the mastaba, was no longer visible. I think to solve this problem they built several smaller mastabas on top of the first one.'

This solution to the problem was not, however, achieved all at once. In fact, it took six changes of plan before the Step Pyramid reached its final form. Because at almost every one of these stages, the builders added the finishing touch of facing the local masonry with gleaming white limestone before deciding to build again, it is possible to distinguish the various alterations in places where the pyramid has since subsided. Beginning as a mastaba measuring about 63 m (207 ft) on each side, it soon became a larger and larger mastaba, and only later a monument rising in four levels. The engineering of these levels was perhaps Imhotep's true innovation, and the ultimate result was Egypt's first pyramid: a pyramid comprised of six steps reaching a height of 63.7 m (209 ft), quite visible above the enclosure wall, and a towering symbol of King Djoser's eternal life and power.

In these changes are manifest not only the

Left Dreyer suggests that it was the desire that the king's tomb be visible above the enclosure wall which led to the development of the world's first pyramid.

pharaoh's power, but also his will to create continuously for as long as this life permitted. This is an urge he seems to have inherited from his predecessor. For Khasekhemwy, this desire led to ever bigger and better structures in three different locations. Djoser, on the other hand, concentrated his creative powers in one place with remarkable results.

Not surprisingly, this new type of monument made a strong impression on the Egyptians. Soon the pyramid became not only a resurrection machine for the pharaoh, but also a striking symbol of royal power in this life and the next. Although none of Djoser's successors in the Third Dynasty were able to complete their pyramid tombs, the last king of the dynasty, a ruler named Huni, was successful in erecting some if not all of the eight smaller step pyramids which curiously dot the landscape from Athribis in the Delta to Elephantine at Egypt's southern border. All are essentially similar in size, most being approximately 18 m (60 ft) square at the base, and there is no evidence that any of them served as tombs. Instead they appear to be emblems of royal presence throughout the land. Much like the mound or 'protopyramid' within the funerary enclosure of Khasekhemwy at Abydos, the little step pyramids may have been focal points for posthumous veneration and offerings for the king. However, the distribution of these little pyramids at or near provincial administrative centres suggests that they also had significance during the king's life. It is possible that each of these places once contained a provincial palace for the king's use during his tour of the country for the purposes of tax collection and census counts. This tour took place every other year and in the early Old Kingdom the years of a king's reign were recorded according to the number of times this census and collection took place. How often the king himself actually took part in this process is unknown, but with the enduring symbol of his authority ever-present, his physical attendance may not have been required. The function of these intriguing pyramids is, however, still a matter of speculation. While some have been known for a while, others, like the one at Athribis, have only recently been discovered. Still others that may lie concealed under the sand could prove capable of shedding further light on their true purpose and meaning.

Snefru

The greatest builder of the Pyramid Age was King Snefru, the first king of the Fourth Dynasty, during whose reign the biennial tax levy may have become a more frequent event. As a result, it is difficult to assess the true intensity of Snefru's creative power. He is accorded a reign of twenty-four or twenty-nine years in the ancient king-lists, yet the recent discovery of an inscription mentioning the twenty-fourth occasion of the census suggests he may have reigned as long as forty-eight years, if the taxes were still collected every other year. But regardless of his total years, his reign is distinguished by the number and sheer magnitude of the works he carried out. The owner of

Opposite King Snefru (c.2613–2589 BC) was the greatest pyramid-builder in Egyptian history. Stela from Snefru's 'Bent Pyramid', showing the seated figure of the king.

Left The Bent Pyramid at Dahshur would have surpassed the height of the Great Pyramid had it been completed as designed, but the foundations could not support the weight and the plans had to be changed.

Far Left Snefru's first pyramid at Meidum was originally constructed as a step pyramid. The king later transformed it into a true geometric pyramid.

three full-sized pyramids and probably two smaller ones, he shifted one-third more stone – some 3,600,000 cubic metres (4,708,800 cubic yards) of it – than his son and successor Khufu, the builder of the Great Pyramid.

Snefru's reign represents an important period in Egyptian history, a period of transition in art and architecture. It was a time when developments in the rendering of the human form and major advances in the working of stone were crystallized and perfected. To him belongs the credit for the first geometrically true pyramids ever attempted in Egypt, as well as major and long-lasting changes in how the resurrection machine functioned. It was his experiments with its conception and form that set the stage for the remarkable achievements at Giza.

Previously believed to belong to Huni, simply because no one could conceive of one king building so much, the pyramid at Meidum is now recognized as the first of Snefru's projects. Its bizarre shape, the result of later stone-robbing, has earned it the Arabic name 'Haram el Kaddab' or 'The False Pyramid'. It was, however, built – again after several changes of plan – as a step pyramid, the only full-sized one after Djoser's to have been completed. Snefru then decided to try his hand at something completely different.

For his second great project, Snefru chose the previously unused plateau at Dahshur further to the north. He selected the site for his pyramid, now known as the 'Bent Pyramid', for obvious reasons. Here was a large flat area with good-quality stone near by and a gorge that could serve as a natural transport ramp from the Nile. It appeared to be very suitable place to build a new eternal abode of a great ruler. This turned out, however, to be a crucial mistake.

The underlying sands and shales eventually proved unable to support the weight of the pyramid, the first to be designed as a true geometric pyramid and one that would have surpassed the height of the Great Pyramid had it been completed as planned. Although various theories have been proposed to explain the curious change in angle which gives the Bent Pyramid its name, the most convincing reason for its shape was the necessity to remedy the cracks and fissures caused by subsidence which began to appear even while this pyramid was being built.

Dr Rainer Stadelmann, Director of the German Archaeological Institute, has been studying the pyramid for many years to determine exactly what went wrong. As the Bent Pyramid retains more of its original smoothed outer casing blocks than any other pyramid, it is not easy to discern the ancient problems and the methods used to solve them. The best evidence is actually found on the inside of the pyramid within its internal passages and chambers. By studying the cracks and repairs in these areas, Stadelmann has been able to recreate the unfortunate chain of events.

The original plan was to build a true pyramid with a rather steep slope of about 60 degrees, but about half-way through construction the outer casing began to crack. To prevent further subsidence, additional masonry was added to all four sides, reducing the angle of inclination to 54 degrees. Yet it was too late. Fissures in the blocks of the completed internal chambers appeared. They tried everything: plaster patches, a new lining of masonry, and even imported cedar logs to shore up the walls.

It was clear that drastic measures were necessary to save the pyramid, the largest monumental building attempted since the beginning of the Egyptian state, but what more could they do? Ultimately, the architects decided that a radical reduction of the angle and a change in the method of laying the masonry were required. The upper half of the pyramid was completed at an angle of 43 degrees to a height of 105 m (344 ft) with smaller stones laid in horizontal rather than inwardly sloping courses to diminish the weight of the mass. Then Snefru started again.

Two and a half miles (4 km) to the north lies Snefru's third pyramid. Called the 'Red Pyramid' after the rusty tinge of the local limestone of its core, it would become Snefru's final resting place. Quick to learn from their mistakes, this time the king's architects laid a foundation platform of several courses of fine white limestone to prevent the problem of subsidence from recurring. The lesson of the Bent Pyramid also encouraged them to construct the pyramid with stones laid in level, rather than inclined, courses at the similarly modest angle of 43 degrees to a not insubstantial height of 104 m (341 ft), making it the fourth highest pyramid ever built. With its construction, pyramids left the arena of experimentation and finally achieved the distinctive and proper geometric form they would retain until their building ceased.

The perfection achieved on the exterior of the Red Pyramid is matched by the elegance of its internal chambers. A long descending corridor entered from the north side of the pyramid led to three rooms, over 12 m (40 ft) high and built of enormous limestone blocks. Two connecting chambers were at ground level within the base of the pyramid, but the third was shaped within the masonry of the pyramid itself. It could only be entered via a carefully concealed passage in the wall of the second chamber, some 7.6 m (25 ft) above its floor. According to Rainer Stadelmann, 'With this marvellous sequence of large and high rooms, King Snefru finally had achieved a burial place he could be happy and content with. It was his eternal residence, built with absolute perfection.' The most stunning aspect of these rooms is the corbelled ceilings, the blocks of which were placed in eleven to fourteen layers, each one protruding out over the room about 15 cm (6 in) on all four sides until a pyramid-shaped roof was obtained. In this ingenious way, the weight of the pyramid could be supported. More than two million tonnes of stone rested on these ceilings, yet there are no cracks, no subsidence. Not only had the architects tackled the vexing problems of construction, but by creating a pyramid within a pyramid, they reinforced the king's chances of resurrection.

For over twenty years Rainer Stadelmann has been excavating around the

Below This isometric drawing of the Red Pyramid shows the internal system of three chambers entered by a sloping corridor from the north side.
The temple complex on the east of his pyramids was another of Snefru's innovations.
(After Rainer Stadelmann)

Red Pyramid. His discoveries have added considerably to our understanding of Snefru's reign and vision. But one discovery in particular has helped to answer the age-old question of how long it took to build a pyramid. Stadelmann explains:

> 'When we started excavating here we found part of the outer casing still preserved, but a lot of blocks had fallen or were displaced. On the reverse of these loose stones we found inscriptions in red paint naming the working gangs who constructed the pyramid, for examples, the "Green gang" or the "Western Gang". We also found the name of Snefru in a cartouche. I would say about every twentieth stone was inscribed, but the most exciting thing was that dates were also written on the backs of these blocks.'

From these dates, Stadelmann has been able to determine the sequence of work. An inscription on one of the foundation blocks dates the beginning of construction to the fifteenth census count undertaken during Snefru's reign.

perhaps equivalent to his twenty-second or twenty-ninth year on the throne. Two years later, six layers of stone had been laid. Within four years 15 m (49 ft), or about 30 per cent. of the pyramid were already completed. When studied together. the inscriptions show that it took about seventeen years to construct the entire pyramid.

To celebrate its completion, the proud builders added a solid limestone pyramid-shaped capstone, called today a 'pyramidion'. To the Egyptians, it was the *benbenet*, the very tip of that mound of creation where the creator god stood when he created the world. Placed on top of these soaring mounds of masonry, it joined the earth with the sky. Few pyramidions from the Pyramid Age survive, possibly because many were gilded with precious metals. The earliest one now known was discovered in fragments around the base of the Red Pyramid. After painstaking restoration, Stadelmann found that each side had a slightly different angle; even with all of their experience in construction, the Egyptians had trouble reaching the top without some readjustments. Such mistakes remind us of the human elements in these austere piles; nevertheless, the error is extraordinarily small – only 2 degrees over 102 m (335 ft), almost 160 courses of stone! Such a minimal readjustment is, in fact, a true testimony to the abilities of Snefru's architects.

To complete such a pyramid in seventeen years is an even more impressive feat when one considers that at the same time Snefru was hedging his bets by filling in the steps of the pyramid at Meidum, transforming it too into a geometric pyramid, a shape for which he and his architects deserve full credit. But with this change in shape also came a transformation of the concept of the afterlife and a modification of the complex necessary to ensure it.

The shape and orientation of the pyramid complexes of Snefru's ancestors suggest they looked to the stars, linking their journey to the afterlife with the never-setting circumpolar stars, 'the imperishable ones', as they called them. But while they ascended their staircase to the stellar sphere, Snefru trod a ramp of gleaming white limestone like the sun's rays to heaven. To reinforce this connection Snefru laid out his temples along a new east–west alignment in accordance with the course of the sun. This new emphasis on the sun led to the adoption of an entirely new name, a new manifestation, of the king on his ascension to the throne as the 'Son of Ra', the son of the sun god, a father he would join in the afterlife. Snefru pioneered his new axial design for his resurrection machine at all three of his pyramids, but his son and successors at Giza perfected it.

Giza

Equipped with the accumulated experience of his father Snefru, Khufu concentrated his creative energies at the northern edge of the Giza plateau. His Great Pyramid is remarkable not only for its sheer size, rising some 146 m (479 ft), but also for the extreme accuracy of its orientation and the precision

Opposite Rainer Stadelmann with the reconstructed pyramidion of the Red Pyramid.

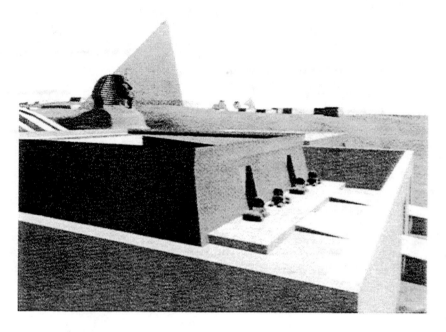

Above The valley temple of Khafra. In the view below, ramps lead from the harbour into the valley temple enclosure. Beside it, the Sphinx and Sphinx temple are unique to Khafra.

of its construction. Despite its undeniable majesty, time has been kinder to its neighbour, the pyramid of Khafra, a structure only 0.6 m (2 ft) smaller. The network of buildings at its base represents the best preserved of all the Old Kingdom pyramid complexes. It is here that the component parts which make up this new type of solar resurrection machine can best be understood, a type which would become the standard.

Above Reconstruction of Khafra's pyramid complex. The pyramid and mortuary temple were linked to the valley temple by a long causeway.

Numerous architectural features define a pyramid complex, but the most prominent are the valley temple, causeway, mortuary temple and of course, the pyramid itself. At the edge of the cultivated plain, probably fronted by a canal or harbour stood the monumental entrance to the complex, which Egyptologists call the valley temple. Khafra's was built of local limestone but encased in colossal granite blocks. Two doors gave access to this portal within

79

Avove The Sphinx presides over the Giza necropolis as the colossal guardian of the horizon, the living image of Khafra reborn as the sun god.

Opposite The false door allowed the spirit of the deceased, whether king or commoner, to come out and partake of the daily offerings placed before it. Royal false doors were made of red granite. Those of non-royal people were usually made of limestone, often, as here, painted red in imitation of granite. From the tomb of Mehu, Saqqara, Sixth Dynasty, c.2300 BC.

which were twenty-three life-sized statues of the king. Connecting the valley temple and the mortuary temple, linking the life-giving waters and the desert plateau, was a covered causeway or entrance corridor almost 495 m (1624 ft) long. The mortuary temple, which abutted the east side of the pyramid, was an elaborate complex of rooms and courtyards which mirrored the king's palace. The principal part was a large open courtyard surrounded by a pillared cloister and shrines in which the king's sacred image was housed. Here the rituals and prayers for the king were performed and the sustenance and offerings due to him were laid out on an altar in the open courtyard lined with brilliant alabaster. From the private chambers deep within the pyramid, where his mummified body lay encased in its granite sarcophagus, the spirit of the king would emerge to partake of these daily offerings via a niched panel called a 'false door'. Often carved out of hard red granite, it copied the panelled door-jamb, lintel, rounded wood support and double-leaved door of domestic architecture. As the sun rose each morning, its rays illuminated the polished white limestone of the pyramid's eastern face, filling the open court of the temple with light, so that the king's spirit was reborn afresh. Sacred boats symbolically docked outside the mortuary temple and alongside

the pyramid were ready to carry him on his journey through the sky. From the reign of Snefru onward, all kings desired to build such a complex. But Khafra added something unique.

This was the Sphinx, which presides over Giza (and art history) as the first colossal royal statue in Egypt. A composite of a lion's body with the king's head, it is a manifestation of Khafra reborn as the sun god, a powerful creature who guards the necropolis as he guards the horizons. Although it seems that the sphinx (or to the Egyptians *shesep ankh* meaning 'living image') and the temple at its base were never entirely completed, this does not mean that they were an afterthought. Both are intimately connected with Khafra's causeway and valley temple, and had been designed together with them. It was not by chance that the knoll of living rock from which the Sphinx was carved was left in place after the stones for the valley temple were quarried. Although the Sphinx's temple may never actually have functioned, it was designed to serve the sun god. Like a giant sun clock with pillars representing the twelve hours of the day and night, it was oriented so that on the spring and autumn equinox, the rays of the rising sun would illuminate its inner sanctum.

What role the architectural features of the pyramid complex played in the actual funeral of the king remains unresolved. Their major purpose for eternity was two-fold: to serve as a palace for a resurrected king, and as a temple to an immortal god. Unlike the buildings surrounding the earlier Step Pyramid, these complexes were not frozen in time, but dynamic and active institutions. But in order to function, they needed both provisions and personnel.

Pyramid Power

To build and maintain the pyramids, an enormous support system must have existed. Production facilities for food, pottery, building materials and supplies, storage depots, and housing for the workmen and those responsible for servicing the pyramid temples were necessary. This is perhaps where we see the true power of the pyramid: as the centre of a vast engine of production and a key element of the redistributive economy that bound people to the king and kept Egyptian civilization alive for a very long time.

Since the reign of Snefru, an entire town was associated with each pyramid, full of people employed to maintain the king's afterlife. New villages and agricultural estates were founded in the hinterlands specifically for supplying the pyramid cult and those who worked for it. This flow of resources from the peripheries to the pyramid, and thus to the very centre of the state, was in large part responsible for making Egypt into the most powerful centralized nation of its time. The organizational skills each pyramid represents are phenomenal. While skilled craftsmen and management staff worked year round, farmers would come from the provinces during the inundation

The Workmen's Bread

Modern techniques are now making it possible to discover how the bread baked in the pyramid workers' village would have tasted. The taste would have depended on the grain used to make it, and this was the job of archaeobotanists such as Mary Anne Murray to find out. Seeds and other botanical material are separated from the dirt, using a flotation tank, a vat full of flowing water. As its name suggests, this is designed to allow the lighter organic material to float to the top as the dirt and stones sink to the bottom. In this way the fragments of barley and emmer wheat ground to make the bread were recovered. Such grain contains little of the gluten that makes modern bread light and crispy. The loaves were baked over an open fire in large bell-shaped pots. Attempts at reproducing the recipe and the seemingly strange baking technique resulted, not surprisingly, in massive cake-like loaves, high in calories and starch, which could have fed several people at one meal. Far more economical than producing any kind of flat bread, by baking this type of bread in pots the Egyptians had developed a way to feed several hundred or even several thousand people quickly and efficiently.

Mary Anne Murray separates the precious botanic material from the dirt using a flotation tank.

Above The low benches and troughs plastered with fine white clay turned out to be part of a fish-processing plant.

period to do the heavy work. It is estimated that in all, some 200,000 people took part in the construction of a pyramid. But until recently it seemed as if all evidence of their existence had inexplicably vanished. In fact, it was simply a matter of looking in the right place.

To the south of the Giza pyramids lies a featureless tract about 15.8 hectares (39 acres) in extent, as yet unengulfed by the sprawling suburbs of Cairo. Here in 1988 Dr Mark Lehner of Harvard University began to uncover unprecedented glimpses at what it really took to build the pyramids. When Lehner first excavated a rectangular building with a series of curious

pedestals along each wall, he thought he had found a simple granary. But when mud sealings, originally from doors, bags and jars, turned up mentioning the *wabet* or embalming place of Menkaura, the builder of the third pyramid at Giza, he knew he had found something more. Yet before he could investigate further, the modern world intruded.

In 1991 a mechanical digging machine gouged out a huge trench to the east of this building. Out of that trench came thousands of pot-sherds dating from the time of the pyramids. When Lehner and his team examined the trench, they found two intact bakeries: the large bell-shaped pots in which the bread was baked still littering the floor. Ancient tomb scenes show offering bearers carrying large conical loaves of exactly the same shape as these pots would have produced.

The bakery was attached to a larger building, the focus of investigation since 1995. Within it, Lehner explains,

> 'we found these very curious low benches and troughs paved very
> carefully with clean desert clay. We had no idea what they were for
> until we started paying very close attention to the last few milli-
> metres of the deposit over the floor. Scraping that back, sometimes
> with Swiss army knives, we found very fragile fibrous deposits that
> turned out to be the gills, fins, cranial parts and vertebrae of fish. So
> we believe we are in a fish processing centre. Somehow these benches
> and troughs were serving to process and dry fish on a very large scale.
> So, at the base of the pyramids, we have loaves and fishes.'

During further examination, the bones were identified as the remains of catfish, a fish particularly abundant in the waters of the inundation, but one not especially prized for its taste. Exquisite scenes of drag-nets teeming with a wide variety of fish being hauled ashore grace the tombs of the nobles of the Pyramid Age, yet the evidence suggests that fish of any type were not considered appropriate offerings for the deceased, perhaps because of their often unattractive odour. However, payment of labourers with fish is well attested. The conclusion seems inescapable: here is the long-sought facility for feeding the army of workmen who built or maintained the Giza pyramids.

Once the construction of the pyramid was completed, the area then became a cemetery for those who stayed on to support the pyramid cult, and further insights into the once unknown lives of these workmen come from this cemetery. A tourist riding a horse around the pyramids literally stumbled across it, her horse's hoof puncturing what turned out to be the intact vaulted roof of a tomb. Crude hieroglyphs scrawled on the false door identified the tomb-owners as Ptah-shepsesu and his wife. Built of mud brick and scraps of stone left over from the pyramid construction, the tomb is not grand when compared to the mastabas of the nobles laid out near their sovereign at the base of the Great Pyramid. Yet it is a mirror of that arrangement, as

Right Built of left-over stone from the pyramid construction, little mounds of creation cover the graves of some of the workmen.

the tombs of those who worked under Ptah-shepsesu are arranged all around his tomb beneath miniature mastabas of their own. Even in death, status no matter how modest was respected. Since 1990, excavations under the supervision of Dr Zahi Hawass, Director of the Giza Plateau, have revealed over 600 smaller graves grouped around the thirty larger tombs of their masters.

These tiny tombs come in a variety of forms: square, stepped, vaulted and domed to evoke a pyramid-like shape. Made of mud, rubble and construction debris, most are less than a few feet square. Some are fitted out with miniature false doors, and in a few, even of the smallest, statues were found, but most are unfortunately anonymous and without grave goods. Buried without the benefit of mummification, which at this period was still a prerogative of the élite, the bones contained in these tombs tell their story of a life which, though generally healthy, was full of toil. Arthritis and degenerative joint disease, particularly in the back, indicate heavy and sustained labour. These people were not slaves, but their ration of bread and fish was probably well earned.

In the slope immediately above, tombs built of dressed stone belong to a wealthier class: their owners bear titles such as Director of the Draughtsmen,

Below Zahi Hawass examines one of the workmen's tombs. It was outfitted with miniature false doors and a tiny courtyard.

Inspector of the Craftsmen, and Overseer of the Masonry. One of the more interesting tombs is that of a man named Nefer-thieth. One wall in his chapel is beautifully carved with scenes of the tomb-owner and his extensive family, and from it we can reconstruct a little bit more of the lives of these intriguing people. Nefer-thieth had two wives, with whom he had eighteen offspring. Although the specific post he held is never clearly stated, his chief wife, Nefer-hetepes, was a weaver, and indeed, a little extra income may have been useful with all those children, eleven of whom were hers. Because of the number of scenes depicting the making of bread and beer, Zahi Hawass

Above The 'Wall of the Crow' separated the sacred precinct of the Giza pyramids from the town of the living that supported them.

believes Nefer-thieth may well have been the supervisor of a bakery. It is perhaps in this capacity that he could have arranged for the fourteen different types of bread and cakes listed on this wife's funerary offering menu to be delivered on special holidays and for eternity.

In its heyday this area south of Giza must have been a hive of activity, although perhaps not all activities were appropriate in the precinct of the god-kings. To separate the sacred from the profane, a huge stone wall was constructed, now called the 'Wall of the Crow'. According to Lehner, 'anywhere else in the world it would be a national treasure. Actually it has been somewhat ignored at Giza because it is dwarfed by the Pyramids and the Sphinx. But it is much bigger than you think.' Clearance of the drift sand against its southern face revealed it to be 10 m (33 ft) high and more than 12 m (39 ft) thick at its base. The gateway alone is 7 m (23 ft) high and capped with three enormous limestone lintels. It may actually be one of the largest surviving gates in the ancient world.

Left The so-called 'Unfinished Pyramid', the first step of a pyramid built of small blocks and covered with gravel. It was originally considered to have been abandoned and never used.

Below Papyrus documents found in the pyramid temple of Raneferef detail the practical workings of the 'resurrection machine'. This document records daily deliveries of produce for the temple and its priests.

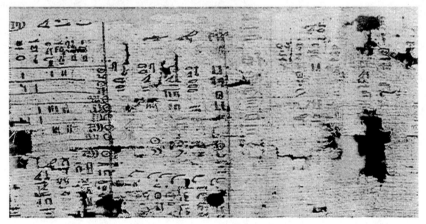

Below Painted limestone statue of King Raneferef (c.2448–2445 BC) discovered in the pyramid mortuary temple.

It will take many more seasons of digging to unlock all the secrets in this unexpected place, but already it offers an exceptional window into the perhaps unremarkable lives of the ordinary people who made and maintained some of the world's most extraordinary monuments. It is not, however, the only source of information available to us on this subject.

Abusir

At Abusir, not far to the south of Giza, the tombs of kings of Egypt's Fifth Dynasty (c.2494–2345 BC) are the 'Forgotten Pyramids'. Robbed of their fine limestone casing in the Roman Period, they cannot compete with their

Above Excavations at the base of the 'Unfinished Pyramid' revealed an extensive mortuary temple dedicated to the afterlife of the short-lived King Raneferef.

colossal neighbours, yet it is here that unique documentary evidence for how the pyramids functioned was found.

In 1893 local farmers digging in the ruins stumbled across over 300 fragments of papyrus from the pyramid complex of King Neferirkara (*c.*2475–2455 BC), which were then sold and distributed around the world. This unique archive contained the duty rosters of the pyramid temple personnel, inventories of the pyramid's equipment, accounts of its income and even reports on inspections of its physical condition over the years. Yet this extraordinary collection, written in ink in hieratic (a cursive form of the hieroglyphic script), remained unpublished for seventy-five years.

89

As a result, the first archaeologists to excavate at Abusir did not have the benefit of these documents to guide them. However, the Czech mission which has been exploring the site since 1976 has made full use of them. One scrap in particular caught the attention of Professor Miroslav Verner, director of the Czech Mission. It mentioned the mortuary temple of a little-known king, Raneferef (*c.*2448–2445 BC), whose tomb had never been found. Verner immediately realized it meant that this king's tomb and temple must be somewhere at Abusir, but where? The logical place to begin was at the so-called 'Unfinished Pyramid', the lowest step of a pyramid core which was believed to have been abandoned unoccupied. Using sub-surface sensing techniques, the Czech archaeologists were amazed to discover that a complete and once active mortuary temple had been built in front of this unfinished pyramid.

More surprising still was what they discovered when they began excavating this temple. Amongst the tumbled walls was the largest cache of Fifth Dynasty royal sculpture in existence, including a fine painted limestone statue of King Raneferef, his head shielded by his protector, the falcon god Horus. But this was not all: gratifyingly, another collection of rare papyrus documents detailing the working of this king's temple cult were uncovered.

It seems that King Raneferef died prematurely, when the underground chambers of the pyramid were complete but only the lowest step of the superstructure constructed. What happened next provides a revealing insight into how the Egyptians viewed the workings of a resurrection machine. After his death, his successor Niuserra (*c.*2445–2421 BC) quickly turned the unfinished pyramid into a makeshift mastaba, encasing it in fine limestone and topping it with gravel – it is little wonder that it is called 'the mound' in the contemporary papyri. To it he attached a mortuary temple for Raneferef's

Right The priests' duties were to assist in the daily rituals and to help transport, maintain, guard and inventory the provisions and possessions of the pyramid complex. Relief from the tomb of Ankhmahor, Saqqara, showing offerings being brought for the consumption of the deceased. Sixth Dynasty, c.2300 BC.

Above Miroslav Verner directs the clearance of the burial shaft. He hopes that some remnant of Raneferef's funeral equipment may still be found.

eternal nourishment. Originally of mud brick and fitted-out with the bare necessities of a red granite false door and an altar, the mortuary temple was later enlarged into a sprawling complex of halls, courts, storerooms and even a slaughterhouse called the 'Sanctuary of the Knife'. Although burial beneath a pyramid was every king's ideal, each king clearly had to build his own. For those unlucky enough to die before completing theirs, a lesser mound of creation would suffice, but for the practical business of resurrection a working mortuary temple was indispensable.

The Abusir documents give us a detailed picture of how these mortuary temples worked. We now know that, in addition to a permanent staff of priests, purifiers and scribes, each mortuary temple was manned by a team selected from a cross-section of the inhabitants of the associated pyramid town. The higher-status members were called 'servants of the god', while the others were simply referred to as 'those before the irrigation basin', or townsfolk. This non-permanent priesthood was divided into five groups called by Egyptologists *phyles* or tribes. There were perhaps forty priests per phyle and they were subdivided into two groups of twenty. Each sub-group served in the temple one month in ten. This system allowed a large number of people to be involved in and benefit from the service of their departed sovereign.

The duty of these priests was to assist in the daily rituals for the king and to help transport, maintain, guard and inventory the possessions and provi-

Opposite The burial chamber of King Unas (c.2375–2345 BC), the walls inscribed with the first ever 'Pyramid Texts', the oldest religious literature in the world.

sions of the pyramid complex. Some were so punctilious at their job they recorded even the fact that a ball of incense was not in its proper place in a box. Each morning and every evening the sacred rites took place. Before the royal statues, the ceremony of re-animation called 'the opening of the mouth' was performed (see page 209). The townsfolk would unveil, bathe and dress the statues, while the servants of the god chanted the sacred formulae and fumigated with incense. Now the king's spirit was ready for the ritual meal. The documents reveal that the king enjoyed an extensive menu, and so did the priests. For once the king's spirit had partaken of the essence of the offerings, the priests partook of their physical presence. There seems to have been plenty to go around: according to one papyrus from the archive of Raneferef, 130 bulls were slaughtered in the course of just one ten-day festival – all this to honour a relatively short-lived king.

In effect, the pyramid complexes functioned as part of a massive redistribution scheme and one that was highly successful. As at the pyramids of other more important kings, Raneferef's cult was maintained until the end of the Old Kingdom and was then revived briefly in the Middle Kingdom 400 years later. Far from sapping the resources of Egypt, the pyramids nourished the nation as well as the king's spirit.

As long as the mortuary temple was up and running, the king's resurrection and successful afterlife were assured. But the last king of the Fifth Dynasty took out an additional insurance policy.

Pyramid Texts

Lavish and colourful reliefs embellished the walls of the pyramid temples and the causeway, but within the pyramid itself the burial chamber of every king, with the exception of Djoser, had remained unadorned. King Unas, the last king of the Fifth Dynasty, changed all that. Erecting his pyramid at Saqqara, directly adjacent to the Step Pyramid complex of Djoser, he followed his neighbour by decorating his internal chambers, but in an entirely new way.

Around his black basalt sarcophagus, evocative of the fertile earth, he placed white alabaster slabs incised and painted to resemble the matting of a divine purification tent, open to a sky in the form of a gabled ceiling decorated with golden stars against a field of deep blue. Intricately carved all around this were the words of the oldest religious literature in the world. Called the Pyramid Texts, they are spells and ritual utterances drawn from a body of sacred knowledge, some immeasurably old and others newly invented. Some are spells to keep away danger, to protect the king from noxious snakes and insects; others are tabulations of the food, drink and clothing required for eternity. Some are hymns to the gods and litanies of their sacred names. But others, complete with instructions for words to be spoken or ritual actions to be performed, must have been incantations recited at the king's funeral and during the daily ritual in the pyramid temple. Together

Left The tomb of Thutmose I (c.1504–1492 BC) was carved deep into the rock in a hidden place in the Valley of the Kings.

they chart the journey of Unas into the afterlife, free from misdeed, able to fly past all obstacles to the sky, where his homecoming is celebrated by the gods among whom he thrives for all eternity.

The arrangement of the spells within the pyramid chambers has long been a puzzle. Some scholars think it might reflect the order of the funeral ritual performed over the body of Unas, but a new interpretation suggests that Unas arranged his spells for him to read himself. As added insurance in case the ritual cycle in the pyramid temples should break down, Unas, rising from his sarcophagus, and moving with the spells out to the east toward the sunrise, could transform himself into an effective and immortal spirit.

The kings who followed also made use of this body of texts, sometimes choosing different spells and creating new ones. In all, over 700 different spells are known and no two pyramids contain the same selection. Over the centuries these spells were adapted to changing conceptions and modified to serve the needs of a wider audience. Eventually, inscribed on a papyrus roll and called 'The Spells for Going Forth by Day' or today the Book of the Dead (see page 179), they would become a potent guide for negotiating the afterlife and attaining resurrection for anyone who could afford a copy.

End of the Pyramid Age

The Old Kingdom was the great age of pyramid building in Egypt. Pyramids would continue to be built for another 500 years, but priorities were changing. At the beginning of the New Kingdom, the pyramid form was turned over to the officials of the realm to build over their rock-cut tombs. The king had different plans.

In about 1500 BC King Thutmose I instructed his architect, Ineni, to build him a different kind of tomb. On the west bank of the Nile opposite Thebes, Egypt's most important religious centre in the New Kingdom, he found the perfect spot: a deep canyon dominated by a more enduring monument, a huge pyramid-shaped mountain, today called el-Qurn. Even more compelling, this peak and the massif of which it was a part, when viewed from the city of the living, resembled the hieroglyphic sign for the horizon, specifically the western horizon and the entrance to the underworld. Behind it was the perfect place to build a city of the dead. Here Ineni burrowed deep into the rock; long stepped corridors spiralled down to a burial chamber, a winding way symbolic of the landscape of the underworld. Certain that the body of his pharaoh would be secure, he left a touching inscription on the walls of his own tomb at Thebes. It reads, 'I supervised the excavation of the tomb of His Majesty alone, no one seeing, no one hearing.'

Nearly thirty pharaohs would eventually be buried in what is now known as the Valley of the Kings. At the edge of the cultivated fields each king built his palace of eternity, or Mansion of Millions of Years as it was called, reviving a tradition dating back to Egypt's first kings.

Above Royal pyramids ceased to be built in the New Kingdom. Instead the pyramid-shaped mountain called el-Qurn towers over the royal burial ground of the New Kingdom in the Valley of the Kings at Thebes.

95

Immortality was now reinforced by the stunning array of texts and pictures which decorated their distant tombs and was assured in the increasingly elaborate mortuary temples and temples of state, where the king was portrayed both with and as the god Amun–Ra, the chief god of Thebes. These new mounds of creation, embellished with the tribute from a far-flung empire, would become the focus of the king's creative urge, and would now speak of his power and the glory. And like the pyramids, they continue to stun and amaze.

But this is far from being the end of the story. Centuries later the royal pyramid would make a dramatic reappearance, this time not in Egypt but much further south in Nubia (in present-day Sudan), in a kingdom known to the Egyptians as Kush — until recently one of history's best-kept secrets.

Below View of Gebel Barkal from the south with its distinctive pinnacle at one end. It was called 'the pure mountain' by the Egyptians, who believed it to be the home of a southern, ram-headed manifestation of Amun–Ra, their pre-eminent god and the source of all kingship.

The Pyramids of Kush

The story of the pyramids of Kush goes back to the New Kingdom, to when Egypt had a great empire abroad. For centuries Egypt had coveted the wealth of Nubia, the homeland of the Kingdom of Kush; it had vast resources of gold and other minerals, and dominated the principal trade routes into the heart of Africa. In the Eighteenth Dynasty the Egyptians invaded Nubia, and after a protracted struggle conquered the first Kingdom of Kush (see Chapter

Below Tim Kendall in the rock-cut temple built by King Taharqo directly beneath the pinnacle of Gebel Barkal. The scene on the wall shows the ram-headed Amun–Ra seated within 'the pure mountain'. Kendall points at the uraeus represented as rearing from the mountain's front.

3, Age of Gold). Under King Thutmose I (1504–1492 BC) the Egyptians sacked and burned the Kushite capital, then located at Kerma near the Third Cataract, and under Thutmose III (1479–1425 BC) extended their control southwards to the Fourth Cataract. Here, on the site of an old Kushite settlement, they founded a new city called Napata, which marked the southernmost point of their occupation of Nubia. Napata was strategically located at a point on the Nile where several important desert roads converged. Of even greater significance was the presence near the site of a sacred mountain, one of the Nile Valley's most spectacular landmarks. Known today as Gebel Barkal, the Egyptians called it 'the pure mountain'.

Standing in the desert about a mile from the north bank of the Nile, Gebel Barkal is a flat-topped sandstone outcrop, over 91.4 m (300 ft) high,

its most distinctive feature a soaring free-standing pinnacle on its west corner, itself 82 m (270 ft) high. Beneath the sheer southern face of the mountain are the remains of a large number of temples built and rebuilt, over a period of over 1500 years, by Egyptian and later Kushite kings. Gebel Barkal was clearly a very sacred place, but why? Recent work on the site and its temples by Dr Tim Kendall of the Museum of Fine Arts, Boston, has gone a long way to addressing the question. Kendall believes the answer lies in the

shape of the mountain, in particular in the form of the pinnacle. He points out that inscriptions of Thutmose III from the site indicate that the Egyptians saw Gebel Barkal as a symbol of the primeval mound of creation and the dwelling-place of a southern version – ram-headed – of their state god, Amun–Ra of Thebes. He believes they were first led to this idea by the peculiar shape of the pinnacle:

> 'When the Egyptians came here, they saw in this strange rock formation the image of a very familiar symbol, a rearing cobra or uraeus, the symbol of kingship which the kings wore on their crown. The cobra seems to be wearing the White Crown of the south, symbolizing kingship over the south. So they believed the great god, Amun–Ra of Karnak, the source of all kingship, lived here inside the rock in an alternate form, conferring kingship over the south and the authority to rule over Nubia.'

Opposite Head from a colossal standing statue of King Taharqo, the greatest of the Kushite kings. Made of grano-diorite. From Gebel Barkal.

Thus, conveniently for the Egyptians, they had divine sanction for the conquest and occupation of Nubia. The latter had always really been part of Upper Egypt. The Egyptian king, traditionally 'the lord of the Two Lands', was now legitimately the lord of Egypt and Nubia. Ironically, this formulation was later to rebound on the Egyptians, when the reverse situation occurred – the authority of Amun–Ra of Gebel Barkal being invoked to legitimize Kushite rule over Egypt.

After a hiatus of several hundred years, during which the Egyptians abandoned Nubia, a new independent kingdom of Kush arose during the eighth century BC, its capital at Napata, its cult-centre at Gebel Barkal devoted still to the worship of Amun–Ra. The native kings, proclaiming themselves the true heirs of Thutmose III and other great pharaonic ancestors, laid claim to the throne of Egypt, which they conquered under King Piye (c.747–716 BC) and ruled for over fifty years as Egypt's Twenty-fifth Dynasty.

The most famous and powerful of Piye's successors was King Taharqo (690–664 BC), whose reign marks the high-point of Kushite empire and achievement. Taharqo was a great builder, erecting temples, shrines and statues throughout the Nile Valley, and turning Gebel Barkal into an architectural showpiece, its central temple a southern version of Karnak in Thebes, though on a smaller scale. High up on the great pinnacle he had an inscription recording his dominance carved in hieroglyphs and sheathed in gold – to be visible far and wide, no doubt a spectacular sight as it glistened in the sun. Directly beneath the pinnacle he had another, smaller temple hollowed out of the rock, which contains scenes of the king offering to the gods, one of which confirms Kendall's view of the religious meaning of the mountain and the pinnacle. The scene shows the king standing before a representation of Gebel Barkal. It is painted reddish brown, like sandstone, and has a flat top with a sloping front, attached to which is a large rearing uraeus. Within

Overleaf The remains of the main temple dedicated to Amun–Ra, seen from the top of Gebel Barkal. First constructed by the Egyptians in the Eighteenth Dynasty, it was rebuilt and extended by the Kushite kings to be their 'southern Karnak'.

99

Opposite The pyramids
of Nuri. King Taharqo's prominent
among them.

it sits the ram-headed Amun–Ra. The accompanying inscription, in
Kendall's words,

> 'actually tells us that he's in the mountain, that he's Amun–Ra, lord
> of the thrones of the Two Lands, who is in the pure mountain,
> which is what they called Gebel Barkal, and you see how they rep-
> resented the pinnacle as a giant rearing cobra with a sun-disc on its
> head...the way they imagined it from the west side of the
> mountain.'

Below Pyramid-fields at Meroe.
In the foreground lies the
southern cemetery; in the
distance, the northern. There is
also a western cemetery. Together
they contain the remains of over a
hundred pyramids.

Seeing themselves as the restorers of order after a period of chaos, the
Kushites, while enthusiastically embracing pharaonic iconography, sought
models – for their art, architecture and rituals – in the hallowed past, at the
same time imparting to them a distinctive style of their own. The most
prominent of their revivals was the pyramid – a tomb form long abandoned
in Egypt. Beginning with King Piye, a new period of pyramid building was
inaugurated, which, astonishingly, was to last for over a thousand years, sur-

viving not only the expulsion of the Kushites from Egypt in about 662 BC but also the move of their royal cemetery from Napata to Meroe in the south just after 300 BC. During this period an extraordinary number of pyramids was erected, both around Napata, at the cemeteries of El Kurru, Nuri and Gebel Barkal, and in Meroe, which contains the largest single concentration of pyramids in the Nile Valley. The total number of Kushite pyramids known to date is 223, far exceeding the number attested from Egypt, though they are, of course, in general much smaller and not all are royal, since the privilege of owning a pyramid-tomb was extended in due course to members of the private élite.

The largest of the Kushite pyramids, by some distance, is Taharqo's at Nuri, which in its final, enhanced form stood to a height of over 49 m (160 ft) and is thought to have been inspired by the pyramids of the Old Kingdom near Memphis. More typically, Kushite pyramids are relatively slender with steep sides, sometimes with moulded edges. Unlike their Egyptian counterparts, they do not end in a pyramidion but have truncated tops surmounted by an angular capstone. In their finished form, they were covered in white plaster, sometimes painted red and white, with a band of stars around the base and with circular plaques made of blue faience inserted in their surface. The earlier pyramids are built throughout of stone, while the later examples, like those at Meroe, consist of a core of debris enclosed by a stone casing; some of the very latest are made of red brick or just rubble.

The most important pyramids in Meroe are those of the so-called northern cemetery, which was reserved for the exclusive use of the royal

Right The northern cemetery
at Meroe, a royal burial ground
which includes the pyramids of
thirty kings and eight ruling queens.

Above Workmen of the
Sudanese Antiquities Service in
the process of reconstructing one
of the pyramids in the northern
cemetery, using a lifting-device
called a *shaduf*.

family. Thirty kings, eight ruling queens (called *kandake* – the origin of the modern name Candace), and three princes or co-regents were buried there. The exact methods of building these pyramids have recently been investigated by the German architect Friedrich Hinkel, who worked with the Sudanese Antiquities Service to stabilize and reconstruct a number of them. Quite unexpectedly, in four of them he discovered the remains of a vertical post, made of cedar-wood, which he believes functioned as the shaft of a giant *shaduf*, a traditional lifting device commonly employed in the Nile Valley for raising water for irrigation, here adapted for lifting stone blocks for the casing of the pyramid. To prove the point Hinkel reconstructed one of the pyramids using just such a *shaduf*. It worked perfectly. Based on his experiment, Hinkel has been able to determine that the steep incline of the sides follows necessarily from the use of the *shaduf*, and that to erect one of the larger pyramids, standing to a height of about 30.5 m (100 ft), would have taken about a year.

Unlike many of their Egyptian predecessors, these pyramids were never intended to house a burial within their structure. They marked the presence of a tomb, rather than being the tombs themselves. The burial chambers, accessed directly from above or from the east by means of a descending staircase, are always subterranean. These different elements were not built concurrently but represent quite separate phases in the construction process. In some cases, the owner of the pyramid built only the underground chamber, in which he or she was buried; the construction of the pyramid itself was begun only after the funeral and was the responsibility of the successor, who was also duty bound to complete the remainder of the mortuary complex. The most important element here was the cult chapel on the east side, decorated internally, in egyptianizing mode, with scenes of the deceased in the company of various funerary gods, giving and receiving offerings. From the outside, the chapels, fronted by pylons (towers flanking a temple gateway), look like miniature temples. They too, like the pyramids, were plastered and painted.

The occupants of the tombs were buried with the traditional rich trappings of royalty, though only fragments and scraps of their original contents have survived, almost all the burial chambers having been thoroughly plundered in antiquity. Externally the pyramids remained in very good condition until the nineteenth century, when they were subjected to the

Right and opposite Jewellery, in the form of an armlet and a shield-ring, from the treasure of Queen Amanishakheto (late first century BC), found in her tomb in the northern cemetery at Meroe. Made of gold with glass inlay, the decorative technique and style, combining Egyptian and Kushite motifs and insignia, are typically Meroitic. The central motif on the shield-ring is the head of the Kushite lion god, Apedemek. On the armlet is the Egyptian funerary goddess Isis.

most appalling damage. In 1834 an Italian adventurer, Guiseppe Ferlini, began to dismantle some of them, searching for hidden treasure. He struck lucky, finding a collection of stunning gold jewellery in the pyramid or tomb of Queen Amanishakheto, who ruled in the late first century BC. It is the largest and most important cache of Meroitic jewellery ever discovered, containing many rare items and types otherwise known only from representations. All are wonderful examples of the goldsmith's art, their complex iconography, combining Meroitic, Egyptian and Hellenistic motifs, bearing eloquent testimony to the cosmopolitan world that the Kushites inhabited. Tragically, the discovery sparked a great wave of treasure hunting. The pyramids were systematically vandalized and some almost totally destroyed.

Today, the ruined pyramids of Meroe form one of the most evocative and poignant landscapes to have survived from antiquity. Including in their midst the last pyramid ever built on the African continent – erected in AD 370 and now reduced to a humble heap of rubble – they mark the end of an awesome tradition, one which survived for over 3000 years and has given the world its most enduring symbol of the ancient past.

Right Head of a figure of Amun–Ra, the king of the gods, made of solid gold, the 'flesh of the gods'. Probably a cult statue from a temple shrine. From Thebes. New Kingdom–Third Intermediate Period, c.1400–850 BC.

Far right Scene showing Nubians – chiefs, princes and a princess – doing obeisance and bringing gold to to the Egyptian court. From the tomb of Huy, Viceroy of Kush under King Tutankhamun, Thebes, 1336–1327 BC.

AGE OF GOLD

Left Gold bracelets inlaid with carnelian, turquoise and blue frit, inscribed with the name of King Thutmose III. Part of the jewellery buried with three of his queens. From Thebes. Eighteenth Dynasty, c.1450 BC.

uring the New Kingdom (1550–1069 BC), and especially the Eighteenth Dynasty (1550–1295 BC), the Egyptians ruled a great empire, stretching northwards into the Near East as far as the Euphrates and southwards deep into present-day Sudan, to the Fourth Cataract of the Nile and beyond. It was an empire forged initially by military might but sustained in the end by diplomacy and the gift of gold. The most beautiful and precious

of all materials, gold was universally sought-after, and Egypt was its main source. Egypt had access to seemingly inexhaustible supplies, from the deserts east of the Nile Valley and from Nubia. In Egypt gold was reputed to be as 'common as dust'.

But gold was not simply a precious commodity. It was valued by the Egyptians for reasons beyond its intrinsic worth. The colour of the sun, untarnishable, unaffected by time, gold was a symbol of eternity. Transformed by ritual, gold became the flesh of Ra and the other immortal gods. To be bedecked with gold was to partake of its divine qualities, and to be buried with gold – ideally wearing a gold mask, encased in gold coffins, like Tutankhamun

(1336–1327 BC) – was to be ensured eternal life. In royal tombs, the burial chamber was known as the 'house of gold'.

In the New Kingdom, the Egyptians acquired, buried and disbursed gold in unprecedented quantities and enjoyed unparalleled wealth, power and prestige. The age of empire was a golden age in every sense. Yet it had sprung from very inauspicious circumstances, during a period when Egypt, for the first time in its long history, was ruled by foreigners.

The Hyksos and the Theban Revolt

Following the collapse of Egypt's Middle Kingdom, the country had fallen under the domination of the so-called Hyksos, 'foreign rulers', who held sway for over a hundred years during the Second Intermediate Period (c.1650–1550 BC). Originally immigrants into Egypt from Canaan, the Hyksos had forged a strong power-base in the northeast Delta, an area of great strategic importance, where they established their capital, Avaris (called *Hwt-waret* in Egyptian texts). From this stronghold they were well-placed to control the lucrative trade routes, by land and by sea, with the Near East and the Mediterranean world. To secure their southern border and trade with Africa, they formed an alliance with the powerful kings of Kush, who from their capital at Kerma near the Third Cataract ruled the gold-rich land of Nubia.

Above Stela of King Kamose, which commemorates a successful Theban campaign against the Hyksos king Ipepi. From the Temple of Karnak, Thebes. Seventeenth Dynasty. c.1555 BC.

Right Base of a scarab, decorated with a scene of King Thutmose I standing in a horse-drawn chariot and slaying a foreign enemy with an arrow shot from his great bow. The horse, chariot and composite bow were originally foreign imports into Egypt, but during the New Kingdom they became standard elements in the iconography of the Egyptian king as all-conquering hero.

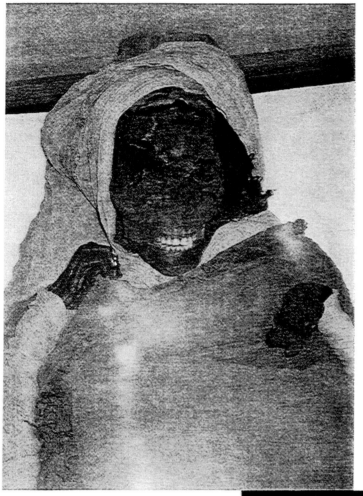

The whole of Egypt paid obeisance to the Hyksos overlords but with increasing reluctance and disaffection, especially in Thebes in Upper Egypt. Here a family of local rulers eventually rebelled, styling themselves as the true kings of Egypt – known to us as the Seventeenth Dynasty (c.1650–1550 BC) – and began a war of independence.

Initially the Hyksos had a substantial advantage in the form of better weaponry and superior military technology. They had the horse and chariot, giving them greater mobility, and a new type of bow, the 'composite' bow, of laminated construction and of great tensile strength, which could shoot arrows over a much longer distance than an ordinary wooden bow. Nevertheless, learning and adapting, the Thebans turned the tables on their erstwhile masters, with such success, in fact, that the horse-drawn chariot and the composite bow, both of foreign origin, soon become icons of Egyptian military dominance, of the pharaoh as the all-conquering hero. But the road to liberation was far from smooth, and at least one Theban king appears to have paid with his life. A mummy excavated at

Above Mummy of King Seqenenre Tao. The wounds in his skull, made by Hyksos weaponry, are plainly visible.

Right Hyksos battle-axe, with cast socket and narrow chisel-shaped blade: a formidable piercing weapon. Second Intermediate Period. c.1650–1550 BC.

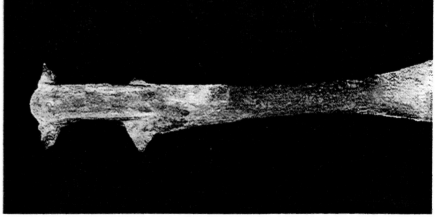

Thebes, now in the Cairo Museum, belongs to King Seqenenre Tao (c.1560 BC), one of the first Theban rulers actively to oppose the Hyksos. The king bears wounds in his skull, which to judge from their shape, were made by weapons peculiar to the Hyksos, one of them a distinctive chisel-shaped battle-axe. It is very probable he was slain in battle.

Greater success was enjoyed by Seqenenre's successor, King Kamose

Above Excavations in progress at Tell el-Daba/Avaris, here uncovering a palatial complex of the early Eighteenth Dynasty, previously hidden underneath the cultivation.

(c.1555–1550 BC). A famous commemorative inscription, the Kamose Stela, gives an account of a Theban campaign led by Kamose against the Hyksos king Ipepi, from which was brought back much valuable plunder, including chariotry and battle axes. Kamose boasts of taunting Ipepi before the walls of Avaris:

> 'Behold, I have come, I am successful...As the mighty Amun endures, I will not leave you alone, I will not let you tread the fields without being upon you. O wicked of heart, vile Asiatic, I shall drink the wine of your vineyard...I lay waste your dwelling place, I cut down your trees.'

But where exactly were the walls of Avaris? And how great a stronghold really was it? For a long time it was impossible to answer these questions. Avaris was a lost city, its precise location unknown, its remains hidden beneath deposits of Nile silt and modern cultivation. The only evidence for its existence was its mention in Egyptian texts – that is until recently, when an Austrian expedition, led by Professor Manfred Bietak of the University of Vienna, in one of the most important archaeological discoveries of modern times, finally located the site of Avaris, in the eastern Nile Delta near a modern village called Tell el-Daba.

Though the city is much ruined, systematic excavation over a period now of more than twenty years has slowly but gradually revealed its infrastructure – its houses, palaces, tombs and temples – and shown how it changed and developed through time. Beginning as a small Egyptian settlement in the Middle Kingdom, Avaris was gradually occupied by an increasingly large and thriving Canaanite community, eventually emerging as a great cosmopolitan city, the capital of the Hyksos, in the Second Intermediate Period. The work has shown that at its zenith Avaris was even more formidable than we might have imagined. Extending over an area of 0.96 square miles (2.5 sq. km), it was one of the largest cities in the eastern Mediterranean world, an international centre of commerce and trade. Bietak estimates that scattered over the

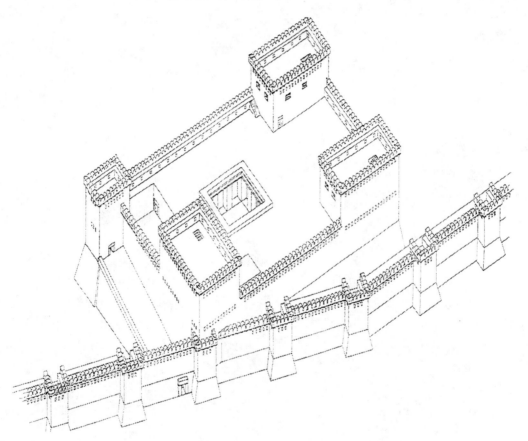

Above Reconstruction of the palatial fortress of the early Eighteenth Dynasty, built on the site of the earlier Hyksos citadel. *(After Manfred Bietak)*

site are the remains of over two million pottery containers for imported wine, oil and other commodities.

We now know that Avaris was defended by an impressive buttressed wall, made of mud brick, over 8 m (26 ft) thick, and a huge fortified citadel, which had been strategically located at a bend in one of the ancient Nile channels, now disappeared. Associated with the citadel was a garden for growing vines, the very vineyard, Bietak believes, threatened with appropriation by Kamose. Confirming the testimony of the Egyptian texts, the archaeology shows that the citadel was abandoned at the end of the Hyksos period and was subsequently modified by the Egyptians in the early Eighteenth Dynasty. That the culture of the inhabitants was indeed Canaanite or western Asiatic is clearly indicated by the style of architecture of the temples and palaces, by the nature of the burial customs, and by the types of artefact found in the graves. Many of these graves belonged to warriors, who were buried with a set of weapons, distinctive among them the form of battle-axe from which Seqenenre Tao received his fatal wounds.

The Desert Routes

A major goal for the Thebans would have been to prevent a military alliance between the Hyksos to their north and the kingdom of Kush to the south. They appear to have thwarted this threat by carrying out a pre-emptive strike against the Kushites and by disrupting communications between the two allies. The Kamose Stela recounts that the Hyksos king, Ipepi, had sent a letter to the king of Kush, reminding him of their mutual interests and urging him to launch an attack from the rear while Kamose was occupied in the Delta:

'He [Kamose] chose the two lands to persecute them, my land and yours, and he has ravaged them. Come, navigate downstream, do not be afraid. Behold he is here with me. There is no one who will be waiting for you in this Egypt, for I will not let him go until you have arrived. Then we shall divide the towns of this Egypt, and the land of Khent-hen-nefer [Nubia] will be in joy.'

Right Map showing desert routes and location of major caravan stops in the Qena Bend. *(After John and Deborah Darnell)*

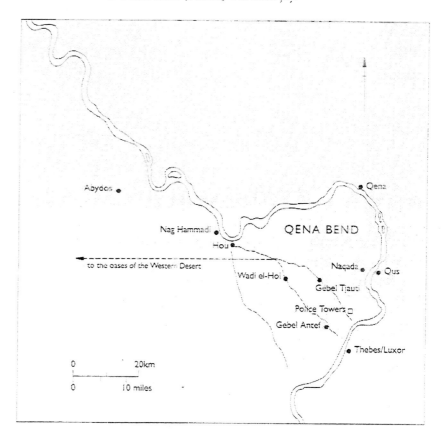

Above John and Deborah Darnell examining petroglyphs (rock inscriptions and pictures) at Gebel Tjauti, assisted by a workman who holds a mirror to reflect sunlight onto a shaded area. This part of the cliff, with its overhang offering welcome shade, appears to have functioned as a regular rest-stop for desert travellers.

Perhaps crucially for the outcome of the war, the letter never arrived, for the messenger carrying it was intercepted on his desert route by one of Kamose's patrols. His capture is unlikely to have been simply a piece of good fortune; more likely it was the result of a deliberate policy by the Thebans of monitoring and policing desert routes.

It is becoming increasingly clear that the Egyptians' use of the desert – for travel, trade and general communication – was much greater than has previously been thought, and that control of the desert routes would have been especially vital during periods of conflict. Important new light on the subject has been shed by two American archaeologists, Dr John and Deborah

Darnell of the University of Chicago, who over the last six years or so have been carrying out a systematic survey of the desert west of Thebes. Their findings have been extraordinary, revealing a hitherto unmapped system of ancient roads, short-cutting the Qena Bend of the Nile and linking with other routes to the great oases in the west and to Nubia in the south. The routes are littered with pot-sherds, of many different periods, showing that they were in heavy use over several millennia. At points along the routes, the Darnells have discovered the sites of major caravan stops, marked by hundreds of rock inscriptions and drawings, left by the travellers.

The inscriptions are written in a variety of scripts, mostly hieroglyphic and hieratic, but also demotic, Coptic, Greek and even Proto-Sinaitic. Typically of such inscriptions, they are not always easy to read and interpret, as they tend to be rather crudely incised and are often superimposed on each other in a confusing manner. To produce an accurate record of the material has taken the Darnells many seasons of painstaking documenting and copying. Concentrated at two sites in particular, in the Wadi el-Hol on the road between Thebes and Hou and at the so-called Gebel Tjauti on the Alamat

Above right Hieroglyphic inscription of the 'police official Aam's son, the overseer of metal workers, Renseneb', incised underneath the rock-hang at Gebel Tjauti, c.1700 BC. It is superimposed on a picture dating from probably nearly 1300 years earlier, while below it are two graffiti in the Coptic script, dating from over 2000 years later.

Tal road, these petroglyphs are far from being simply the ancient equivalents of 'Kilroy was here'; they bear eloquent witness to the many and varied activities in which the travellers were involved and show how busy and important such desert routes were. Many of the petroglyphs are religious in nature, taking the form of prayers to the gods, in particular to the goddess Hathor, who had special significance in the context of the desert. Some commemorate special journeys or events: a royal visit to Thebes or an astronomical observation. Most consist simply of a name and title: among these, policemen, whose task it was to patrol the desert, figure prominently. One of the drawings may well depict a policeman in the process of apprehending a

Above Remains of a watch tower which guarded the Theban end of one the major desert routes and was probably also used as a base for the desert police force.

miscreant. Most important historically, a number of texts testify to military activity and to the strategic importance of those routes. One such text, dating significantly from the Hyksos Period, appears to eulogize a Theban ruler for slaying foreigners in the desert and for striving selflessly to train the desert guards.

This preoccupation with security in the desert is further confirmed by one of the Darnells' most remarkable archaeological discoveries – the remains of two substantial watch towers, 12.2 m (40 ft) in diameter, of rubble and mud brick with drystone ramps along the sides, which guarded the Theban end of the Alamat Tal route and would probably also have served as a base for the roving desert patrols in the region. They were built during the late Second Intermediate Period, the time when the war between the Hyksos and the Thebans was beginning to escalate at the hands of Kamose.

The Beginnings of Empire

Despite his triumphs, Kamose died before he could attain his ultimate goal. The final defeat of the Hyksos and their expulsion from Egypt were to be the achievements of his younger brother, who succeeded him on the throne, Ahmose (1550–1525 BC), the first king of the Eighteenth Dynasty and founder of the New Kingdom. We know this to be the case as the achievement is recorded in a biographical inscription relating to a man who had been a contemporary witness to the events as a serving soldier in King Ahmose's army. The man's name was also Ahmose, son of Ibana, and his biography, one of the longest and most important historical inscriptions to have survived from ancient Egypt, is inscribed on the walls of his tomb at the site of Elkab, his home town in Upper Egypt, south of Thebes. He had a long and distinguished military career, serving under three successive kings, Ahmose, Amenhotep I and Thutmose I, spanning a period of fifty years or so, during which he rose from the junior ranks to be Admiral of the Fleet.

He gives an account of several campaigns, with particular reference to his own acts of bravery – the slaying of enemies and the taking of prisoners – and to the recognition and rewards he received, in the form of gold, slaves and land. The highest accolade that could be bestowed upon a soldier in ancient Egypt was the award of the so-called 'gold of bravery' by the king. Ahmose, son of Ibana, was given this award no fewer than seven times. He must have been one of the great military heroes of his age as well as a very wealthy man at the end of his career. A representation of him in the tomb shows him proudly wearing some of his gold.

Right Limestone figure of King Ahmose, who was responsible for the final defeat of the Hyksos and their expulsion from Egypt. Invading first Canaan and then Nubia, he initiated Egypt's great imperial age, the 'Age of Gold'. From Thebes.

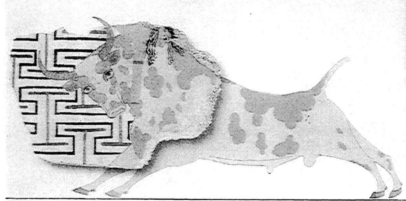

Above Minoan fresco-fragment
showing part of a bull-leaping
scene with a maze pattern in
the background. Such a scene is
otherwise known only from
the royal palace of Knossos in
Crete. Its presence in an Egyptian
royal palace suggests a strong
link between the Egyptian and
Minoan royal courts.
From Avaris/Tel el-Daba.

We are told that four of these acts of bravery for which he was specially
rewarded took place in the war against the Hyksos under King Ahmose, the
first three in battles around Avaris, which was eventually captured and
sacked, and the fourth during the subsequent successful siege of the town of
Sharuhen, a Hyksos stronghold in Canaan, a campaign which laid the foundations for the Egyptian empire in western Asia.

Following the defeat of the Hyksos, Egypt was now unified under a strong
native king for the first time in over a hundred years. But clearly there was no
room for complacency. It has been suggested that King Ahmose feared that
the Hyksos and their allies might eventually counter-attack and as a result

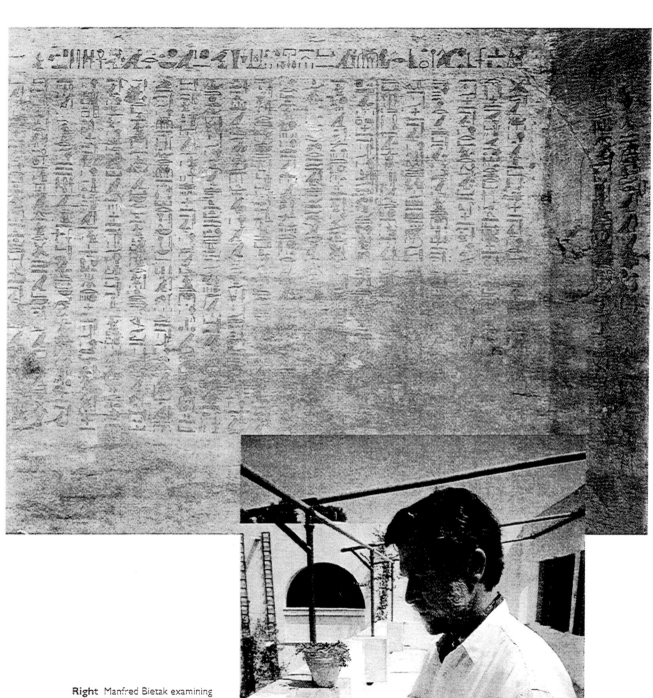

Right Manfred Bietak examining
a fragment from a bull-leaping
scene.

forged an alliance with another great Mediterranean power. The evidence for such a development comes from an astonishing discovery made by the Austrian expedition at the site of the citadel of Avaris – the remains of wall-paintings of superb artistic quality and breathtaking beauty, but completely un-Egyptian in style, content and technique. On close examination, they were recognized as fragments, many thousands in number, of Minoan frescoes, the first ever to be discovered on Egyptian soil. Manfred Bietak believes they once decorated the walls of a new royal citadel, which King Ahmose built on the site of the old Hyksos fortress (see page 114).

The scenes strongly recall the famous frescoes painted on the walls of houses on the island of Thera and in the royal palace at Knossos, the Minoan capital, on Crete – human figures involved in various ritual and sporting activities, including acrobats and bull-leapers, landscapes with plants and animals, including antelope, leopards and lions in flying gallop, and decorative motifs such as rosette-friezes and maze-patterns.

The most important tableau, of which several fragments survive, showed a wonderful scene of bull-leaping. This sport had great ritual significance for the Minoans, expressing, it has been suggested, man's dominance over the power of animals. It is a subject otherwise represented only in the palace at Knossos and appears to have strong royal connotations. The presence of these prestigious Minoan paintings on the walls of an Egyptian palace presupposes a close relationship between the two royal courts, and Manfred Bietak believes that the two powers may well have forged an alliance, cemented perhaps by an inter-dynastic marriage. As the foremost sea-power of its time, Minoan Crete would have provided Egypt with protection against invasion from the sea; in exchange the Minoans would have received gold, African exotica and other luxury commodities, to which Egypt, a growing land-empire, had increasingly ready access.

The Kingdom of Kush

During the Eighteenth Dynasty, gold become a major tool for promoting Egyptian interests and securing important allies. Egypt had some gold mines of its own in its eastern desert, but by far the greatest number and the most productive lay to the south of Egypt, in the eastern deserts of Nubia and along the Nile Valley in the area of the Third Cataract in present-day Sudan. For the new imperial Egypt the possession of those mines became an absolute priority.

With the northern border secured, King Ahmose directed his army southward towards Nubia, most of which was still under the control of the Hyksos' old ally, the ruler of Kush. The roots of the Kushite capital, Kerma, go back to remote antiquity; there is evidence for a settlement in the area as far back as the fourth millennium BC. Subsequently, three major historical phases may be distinguished, each marked by distinctive developments in

Above Reconstruction of the fortified inner city of Kerma, showing clearly the enormous central temple, the *deffufa*, and the conical royal residence of the Middle Kerma Period.

Kerma 2000's

funerary customs and material culture. These phases are known as Ancient Kerma (*c.*2500–2050 BC), Middle Kerma (*c.*2050–1750 BC), and Classic Kerma (*c.*1750–1500 BC). Throughout these periods, Kush was often in conflict with Egypt, resisting the latter's attempts at territorial expansion. Kush proved to be a formidable opponent, its warriors enjoying a legendary reputation for their skills with the bow and arrow. The civilization reached its zenith during the Classic Kerma period, significantly when Egypt was under the rule of the Hyksos.

Though generally portrayed in Egyptian texts as barbaric and of little substance, in reality Kushite culture was highly developed, with a strong and stable economic base and complex political and religious institutions. True appreciation of its nature and achievements has been made possible by the recent excavations of a Swiss team led by Professor Charles Bonnet of the University of Geneva, which has been investigating Kerma, building on the work of a previous American expedition. They have shown that Kerma was no simple settlement, nor, as was once thought, an Egyptian frontier outpost, but a substantial city, the earliest and largest in Africa outside Egypt, which covered at its height a total area of about 26.3 hectares (65 acres).

Right Charles Bonnet examining the beautifully worked marble altar of the *deffufa*.

Below The *deffufa* at Kerma, as it is today, from the west, looking at its main entrance, beyond which a staircase ascends to an altar-chamber, and then to the roof, where open-air rituals were conducted. The temple is made of solid mud brick, its pylons to the right rising to above 20 m (65 ft).

Above View from the roof of the *deffufa* looking south-west. In the foreground are the remains of a large circular hut-like building, believed to have been the royal residence or audience hall during the Middle Kerma Period, c.2050–1750 BC.

Architecturally, it must have been very striking, as impressive in its own way as the contemporary city of Avaris in the north. Its core was surrounded by a massive wall of mud brick, over 9 m (30 ft) high, which had projecting rectangular towers, four fortified gates, and a deep dry ditch in front. This wall enclosed and protected the palace of the king, the houses of the nobility, gardens, and a large religious complex. The centre was occupied by a huge white temple called nowadays the *deffufa* (a traditional Nubian term for any large building made of mud brick), which occupied over 325 sq. m (3500 sq. ft) and whose pylons reached to over 20 m (65 ft) in height – a substantial building even by Egyptian standards. Around it was a secondary religious complex, isolated from the rest of the city by a 5 m (16 ft) high wall, consisting of a number of small chapels, quarters for priests, storerooms and bronze workshops. The great temple, shorn of its white plaster and ravaged by time, is still today a dominating presence, three and a half thousand years after the Egyptians sought the city's destruction.

Above Examples of African products prized by the Egyptians: seen here are logs of ebony, exotic animals and animal skins, a large ivory tusk and ostrich eggs. Thebes, tomb of Rekhmire. Eighteenth Dynasty, reign of Tuthmose III (c.1479–1425 BC).

Above Charles Bonnet and Salah Mohamed Ahmed, Director of Excavations of the National Corporation of Antiquities and Museums of the Sudan, in the dig-house at Kerma, examining a fine ceramic bowl, recently excavated.

At first glance, the *deffufa* resembles an Egyptian temple, but is actually very un-Egyptian in concept and structure. It is a solid mud-brick construction with a single monumental gateway to the side. This entrance gives access to a stairway leading up to a small chamber, which is occupied by a great circular altar of white marble, on which sheep and goats were sacrificed. From the altar chamber, a further staircase, to the left, leads up to the roof, where it is thought that open-air rituals, probably connected with the worship of the sun god, took place. Today, the roof offers a wonderful vantage point from which to view the remains of the city below, the plan and internal organization of which Bonnet has been able to work out in some detail.

One striking vestige, the outline of which can be clearly discerned a little to the southwest, is that of a large round hut, once fitted with a conical roof, whose walls, made of mud brick with wooden supports, stood to a height of at least 9 m (30 ft). A quintessential piece of African architecture, of a scale and type unparalleled elsewhere in the ancient Nile Valley, its size and location suggested to Bonnet that it was the residence or audience hall of the king during the Middle Kerma period. During the succeeding period, a new, larger palace, more elongated and roughly rectangular in plan, was built further to the west and centred on an axis directly aligned with the entrance to the *deffufa*. It was a complex structure, which included a long entrance corridor at the side, storage areas for foodstuffs and other commodities, and an archive room, in which Bonnet discovered the remains of thousands of small mud blanks for making seals, for the marking of goods or sealing of messages, a clear indication that business of some considerable scale was transacted at the site. At the centre of the palace was an imposing audience hall, where the king, seated on a throne placed on a raised platform, received delegations. Its roof was supported by several large columns, estimated to have been about 7.6 m (25 ft) high. This was the palace of the last kings of Kerma. The remains of its walls bear the evidence of burning, and Bonnet believes it was finally destroyed by fire, together with much of the rest of the city, by the invading Egyptian forces led by King Thutmose I (see page 129).

During its heyday, the kingdom of Kerma or Kush controlled not only the gold mines but also major trade routes, both north–south and east–west, with the rest of Africa, from which such highly prized commodities as ivory, ebony, incense, animal-skins and slaves were obtained. It had a sophisticated society, served by highly skilled specialized craftsmen producing a wide range of goods from a variety of different materials. Its most distinctive product was an exquisite pottery, coloured black and red and eggshell thin, among the finest ceramic produced in the ancient world. The kingdom's prosperity

Above Ivory furniture inlays in the forms of animals and birds. From the royal tombs at Kerma. Classic Kerma Period, c.1750–1500 BC. Excavated by an expedition from the Museum of Fine Arts, Boston and Harvard University (1913–1916).

is clear from the wealth of material found in the city's cemetery, which contains over 30,000 burials. During the Classic Kerma period, the kings were buried in huge tumulus tombs over 80 m (262 ft) in diameter, filled with huge quantities of luxury and prestige goods – pottery, jewellery, weaponry, inlaid furniture – mostly of local manufacture but with some Egyptian imports, such as stone sculptures and vessels. Buried with the kings were hundreds of sacrificed animals and human attendants – priests and concubines – to serve them in the afterlife, clear if gruesome testimony to their great status and power. Erected near to the tombs were massive mud-brick chapels (one of them is known as the eastern *deffufa*), where their funerary cults were carried out, the internal chambers finely decorated with faience tiles and painted scenes. The kingdom of Kush was no cultural backwater.

One of the great puzzles surrounding Kush has been the question of how its population and livestock were sustained. To feed the capital city and the population of the kingdom would have required a substantial agricultural base. Yet, most of Kerma's hinterland consists of desert – to all appearances a barren waste punctuated by occasional clumps of trees. Thanks to a recent discovery by a team of archaeologists led by Dr Derek Welsby of the British Museum, however, we now know that this is an entirely misleading picture.

Welsby has been carrying out a detailed survey of the desert region in the Dongola Reach to the south of Kerma for the Sudan Archaeological Research Society. In an area covering about 700 square miles (1813 sq. km), which was previously an archaeological blank, his team has located over 400 ancient sites, settlements and cemeteries, most of them dating from the Kerma Period. When these were plotted on a map, it became clear that many of them fell into a linear distribution, along the banks of what were evidently two old branches of the Nile, still plainly visible in places, where their banks

Below Derek Welsby (on the left) and one of his team, Simon Mortimer, investigate the remains of a stone and timber building, once probably fitted with a raised wooden floor, designed, Welsby believes, for the storage of grain which was destined for the capital city at Kerma. There are many such buildings, dating from the Classic Kerma Period, in this once well-watered area of the Dongola Reach.

are marked by lines of vegetation. Confirming Welsby's results, the northern continuation of these channels has been independently traced by Jacques Reinold of the Sudan Antiquities Service's French Archaeological Unit. Quite remarkably then, what is now desert was once a fertile tract of land, watered by two additional Nile channels. Eminently suitable for the growing of crops and the pasturing of animals, the region supported large numbers of thriving agricultural communities. Significantly, many of the settlements contain the remains of stone and timber buildings, with what may have been raised wooden floors, probably for the storage of grain and other produce. Such buildings are not found in Kerma itself. Welsby believes they may well have formed part of a network of collection points, from which the capital would have been supplied.

But this prosperity did not last, as nature appears to have turned against the kingdom of Kush. The archaeological evidence at present suggests that the two Nile channels began to dry up towards the end of the Classic Kerma period, a change in conditions which would have had serious consequences for the food supply and the viability of the population in the region. If this is the case, it could not have happened at a worse time. Egypt, the colossus to the north, was resurgent, fresh from conquests in Canaan and bent again on southward expansion.

Conquest and the Gold-fields

Beginning with a campaign under King Ahmose, the Egyptian army took Lower Nubia with little resistance. But, despite their internal problems, the Kushites, from their base at Kerma in Upper Nubia, provided stubborn opposition, and it took many campaigns by a succession of Egyptian rulers before they were finally subdued. The decisive blow was struck by Thutmose I (1504–1492 BC), one of Egypt's great imperial kings. Early in his reign, he penetrated to beyond the Third Cataract, the first Egyptian king ever to do so, and inflicted a crushing defeat on a Kushite army. A long inscription, carved on a huge rock at Tombos just north of Kerma, commemorates the victory: 'he has overthrown the chief of the Nubians; none of them has survived. The Nubian archers are fallen in slaughter, are spread over the plains, their entrails fill their valleys, their blood pours down like rain.' It is probable that the sacking and burning of Kerma, witnessed in the charring of its walls, soon followed.

According to his inscription at Elkab, Ahmose, son of Ibana, actually served in the campaign. He speaks proudly of his own feats of bravery in traversing the rapids of the Cataract, as a result of which he was promoted to troop commander. He tells us that Thutmose I himself slew the enemy chief with the first arrow shot from his great bow (see page 110) and that the king sailed back triumphantly to Egypt with the corpse of his enemy hung upside down from the prow of his boat, the arrow still stuck in his chest!

Thutmose I
III
"
Amenhotep III
estab'd
control over
Nubian
goldfields

Having broken the power of Kush, Thutmose I and his successors, especially Thutmose III (1479–1425 BC) and Amenhotep III (1390–1352 BC), firmly established and extended Egyptian control over the Nubian goldfields. The most productive mines were located deep in the Eastern Desert of Sudan, over 150 miles (241 km) from the Nile, in dried-up river valleys or *wadis*, especially the Wadi Allaqi and the Wadi Gabgaba and their tributaries, between the Nile and the Red Sea. Over a hundred mines and goldworking sites are known from these *wadi*-systems. They are currently being explored by an Italian expedition led by Alfredo and Angelo Castiglione. In order to withstand the harsh conditions of the desert, where the days are burning hot and the nights can be freezing cold, this expedition travels in specially designed and equipped vehicles.

Gold occurs in alluvial deposits and in veins in quartz rock. The Castigliones have found plentiful evidence of surface and underground mining for the quartz. They have also found hieroglyphic inscriptions left by ancient Egyptian officials along the routes and at the locations of mines. The

Right The location of gold mines in the Eastern Desert and along the Nile. *(After Vercoutter)*

Overleaf A section of the Wadi Allaqi in the Eastern Desert of Sudan, a region of hugely productive gold mines: in the middle foreground can be seen the remains of buildings belonging to the Graeco-Roman mining town of Berenice Panchrysos.

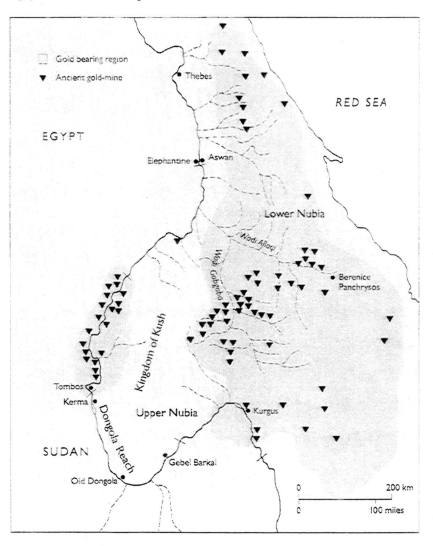

Right Detail of the biographical
inscription of Ahmose, son of
Ibana, from a passage describing
how the chief of the Nubians was
slain by the first arrow shot from
Thutmose I's bow and how his
body was then taken back to
Egypt, hung upside down from the
prow of the king's boat. One of
the hieroglyphs here depicts the
chief upside down, the king's
arrow still stuck in his chest.

Above This large sloping rock,
located near the village of Tombos
at the Third Cataract, bears on its
upper face a long victory
inscription of King Thutmose I,
commemorating his defeat of a
Kushite army. On the rear is a
smaller, later stela of the Viceroy
of Kush, Merymose (see page 136).

Above Gold jewellery, in the form of rosettes, scarabs, flies and arms: part of a robber's loot, dating mainly from the second century BC. From the Wadi Terfowi, a branch of the Wadi Gabgaba.

exploitation of the mines was ruthless and sustained. It is thought that the actual mining was carried out mostly by slaves, prisoners of war and convicts, condemned to hard labour, which many would never survive. Water was in extremely short supply, and we know from Egyptian texts that expeditions might lose substantial parts of their workforce from thirst alone, if they failed to locate or dig wells. The extraction of the quartz must have been backbreaking. Chunks of it had first to be detached and then transported to the surface. Here it was crushed and ground to a fine powder, which was washed with water on a sloping surface to separate the gold. The remains of the implements used by the workers – pestles and mortars and grindstones – are still scattered around in the vicinity of the mines.

The Castigliones have been able to show that the exploitation of these gold-fields continued over centuries. Among their most remarkable discoveries, they have located the site of a long-lost town, Berenice Panchrysos, mentioned by classical writers as a goldworking centre. It is a substantial settlement, one and a quarter miles long (2 km), consisting of two strongholds, administrative offices and houses. The population is estimated to have been at least 10,000. Berenice Panchrysos was the headquarters of the gold industry in this region in the Graeco-Roman and medieval periods. Its

Below Statue of Thutmose III (1479–1425 BC), the grandson of Thutmose I, who extended Egyptian control deep into Upper Nubia. Inscriptions from his reign in the Temple of Karnak at Thebes record the receipt of enormous quantities of gold from Nubia.

existence and its size provide clear testimony of the long productivity of the mines of the Nubian desert.

In the vicinity of the mining sites, the Castigliones have found graves of different dates, some evidently belonging to the native Bedouin who traversed the region and also benefited from its mineral wealth. Hidden in one disturbed grave was a bag containing a tomb-robber's loot – exquisite gold jewellery, including gold scarabs and gold flies, remarkably similar in form to Egyptian jewellery.

Colonial Rule

Enormous quantities of gold poured into the treasuries of the pharaohs from the mines of Nubia. Inscriptions from the time of Thutmose III, the grandson of Thutmose I, record that during three years of his reign an aggregate of 9277 *deben* of gold was received from these sources. A *deben* was a basic unit of weight, equivalent to 91 g (3.2 oz). The total gold recorded is therefore equivalent to 1830 lb (794 kg) weight, worth many millions of dollars at today's prices. These same texts also record the receipt of huge quantities of other much-coveted commodities, such as ivory, ebony, cattle and slaves. Little wonder that the Egyptians were not content merely to conquer Nubia but sought to make it a permanent part of Egypt itself.

As later empires were to do with their subject peoples, the Egyptians cleverly adopted a policy of assimilation and indoctrination. The sons of Nubian chiefs were taken to Egypt to be educated at the Egyptian court and be imbued with Egyptian culture. They learnt the Egyptian language, wore Egyptian clothes, and even took on Egyptian names. Thoroughly 'Egyptianized', they returned to their native land to serve as part of the governing élite in the Egyptian administration.

At the head of the colonial government was a powerful official designated as the Viceroy of Kush, an Egyptian drawn from the pharaoh's inner circle and directly answerable to

him. As 'director of the gold lands of Amun', another of his titles, the viceroy was charged above all with securing a regular supply of that most valued commodity. One of the most famous and successful of these viceroys was Merymose, who served under King Amenhotep III. Merymose's name appears everywhere, most notably in a stela carved on the back of the huge rock at Tombos which bears on the front the great victory inscription of Thutmose I. Here he is pictured with his arms raised in adoration before the names of his master, Amenhotep III. The stela functions as a symbol of the pharaoh's domination and as a tribute to his great ancestor, who had first conquered the region over a century before. Merymose served Amenhotep III as Viceroy of Kush for thirty years. He was ultimately rewarded for his services with a tomb at Thebes, which included, quite exceptionally for a non-royal person, three magnificent hard-stone sarcophagi, beautifully carved with religious scenes and inscriptions.

The long reign of Amenhotep III (1390–1352 BC) was the acme of the imperial age, a period of unparalleled peace and prosperity, which saw great artistic achievements and religious developments. The king initiated a vast building programme, which transformed the architectural landscape of the Nile Valley. He made major additions to the great Temple of Amun–Ra at Karnak, built the magnificent new temple of Luxor, and erected hundreds of statues of the gods and of himself, some of them on a gigantic scale, such as the so-called Colossi of Memnon, which stood in front of his mortuary temple at Thebes. Calling himself 'Egypt's Dazzling Sun', Amenhotep III even aspired to be identified with the sun-god Ra himself, as his embodiment on earth.

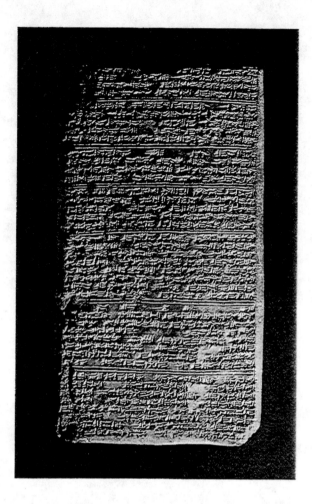

Abroad, the pharaoh's prestige had never been higher. Egypt's wealth was the envy of the ancient world. As we know from the famous cache of diplomatic correspondence called the 'Amarna Letters', rulers great and small wrote to the Egyptian king, pleading for gold, of which Egypt had so much:

'Great King, King of Egypt, my brother... Gold in your country is like dust: one simply picks it up. Why are you so sparing of it? I am building a new palace. Send me as much gold as is required for its adornment.'
(Letter from the King of Assyria to Amenhotep III)

'May my brother send me in very great quantities unworked gold...and much more gold than he sent to my father. In my brother's country gold is as plentiful as dust... Whatever my brother requires for his house, let him write and take it.'
(Letter from the King of Mittani to Amenhotep III)

Above Clay tablet inscribed in cuneiform with a letter from Tushratta, King of Mittani, to Amenhotep III, one of a series detailing negotiations for a marriage between Tushratta's daughter, Tadukhipa, and the Egyptian king. As a bride-price, Tushratta asks for 'gold in very great quantity', adding that 'gold is like dust in the land of my brother'. From Amarna.

In return for gold, the Egyptians were able to acquire prestige commodities, which they coveted but lacked, prominent among them lapis lazuli and conifer wood such as cedar. To judge from the correspondence, foreign princesses were the top of Amenhotep III's list, to swell his harem and strengthen alliances through inter-family marriage.

Houses for Eternity

The élite who served the king well – administrators, priests, soldiers, scribes – shared in the state's wealth and luxury. They were able to commission fine statues of themselves and magnificent tombs. The creation of a tomb, a 'house for eternity', suitably decorated and reflecting their elevated status in life, was every Egyptian's highest aspiration.

The greatest concentration of private tombs belonging to Egypt's imperial age is found carved into the limestone hills overlooking the west bank of the Nile at Thebes. One of these tombs – a particularly interesting one – has recently been the subject of detailed study by Professor Betsy Bryan, Egyptologist and art-historian, of Johns Hopkins University, Baltimore. The tomb belonged to a man called Su-em-niwet, who occupied a high office, that of 'royal butler', under King Amenhotep II (1427–1400 BC). It is one of a

Above Betsy Bryan carefully recording on transparent plastic a painted scene showing the tomb-owner, Su-em-niwet.

group of élite tombs belonging to high-ranking officials of the period which are so positioned in the necropolis as to overlook their king's funerary temple below. It was the custom to decorate the superstructure or chapels of private tombs with coloured scenes, some illustrating the owner engaged in daily-life activities, others showing episodes from his funeral. If the rock in which the tomb was cut was sound enough, the decoration would be carved in relief and then painted; if not, as in the case of Su-em-niwet's tomb, the scenes would be executed in paint on a base of white plaster. Su-em-niwet must have died before his tomb was quite finished, as the painted scenes were abandoned in varying stages of completion. Undesirable as this would have been for an ancient Egyptian, it is what makes the tomb so interesting to modern art historians, as it provides a wonderful opportunity to study painting techniques and methodology, the details of which are largely concealed in a piece of finished decoration.

By close study of the walls, Professor Bryan has been able to determine that a large team of artists, of varying levels of competence, were employed in painting the chapel's three chambers, their work marked by characteristic features of style and technique. She has found that some artists or groups of artists specialized in certain types of composition, some even in certain types of colour. The unfinished state of the paintings has been particularly revealing as to how pigments were mixed to extend the colour range and how compositions were built up, and certain desirable hues achieved, by the careful application of layers of different-coloured paint, placed one upon the other.

The work of one artist, regarded as a true master by Betsy Bryan, stands out from the rest. Interestingly, his work occurs only in the chapel's front chamber – the best-lit in the tomb – and is confined to scenes of a prestigious or unusual nature, for example representations of statues of the king and queen. It is of superb artistic quality, all the more admirable as it was done freehand. In composing a scene, Egyptian artists usually employed a conventional background grid to help them proportion and space the main elements in a scene, but the Su-em-niwet master required no such aid. Using a tiny, slender brush, he drew by eye alone, with enormously practised ease and to wonderful effect, producing perfectly proportioned figures, which he then coloured with great skill and subtlety.

On the other side of the scale is the artistry displayed in the tomb's innermost chamber, the area where the owner's funeral was depicted. Here, in the darkest part of the tomb, the work was assigned to some of the least competent artists, including perhaps apprentices and the more elderly workmen now past their best. One of them worked solely in yellow paint and in a very slapdash fashion: he had no facility to paint consistently to an outline and often obscured or spoiled an otherwise nicely finished detail by covering it with yellow paint. Another kind of error is observable in a depiction of funeral attendants. Closely grouped together, the figures are given different-coloured skins, alternating light and dark red – a commonplace device in Egyptian art for distinguishing between individuals in such contexts. In one area, confusion or lack of attention on the part of the artists has led to two adjacent figures being painted incorrectly, each being shown with a light upper half and dark bottom half.

The growing private affluence of Egypt's imperial age and the increasing demand for finely decorated tombs would have placed a high premium on the services of a master artist. Among other things, Professor Bryan's work has raised questions as to how such artists were recruited for private work. There is no doubt that the very best craftsmen would have been employed in the royal service, primarily in the tombs in the Valley of the Kings. It is possible that some of them might on occasion have been allowed to undertake other commissions for favoured courtiers, or simply did so in their own spare time.

Almost all the kings of the New Kingdom, covering a period of over 400 years, were buried in the Valley of the Kings, from Thutmose I in the early Eighteenth Dynasty down to Ramesses X in the late Twentieth Dynasty. Tutankhamun was buried in a small makeshift tomb, never intended for a king, but otherwise the royal tombs, as befitting the status of their occupants

Opposite Unfinished decoration showing registers of offerings, including military equipment and royal statuettes. The work of a master artist, the scene was drafted free-hand, without the aid of a grid. Tomb of Su-em-niwet; front room, north wall.

and their function as symbolic representations of the great and mysterious underworld, are substantial structures, many times larger and more complex than the contemporary private tombs. Some of them are real giants, the most finished and the finest being the tomb of Seti I (1294–1279 BC), second king of the Nineteenth Dynasty, which is about 100 m (330 ft) long, the walls and ceilings of its many passages, chambers and side-rooms decorated throughout to a uniform standard of excellence. The workmen who built these tombs were not recruited *ad hoc* but were part of a permanent workforce, a select band of craftsmen, specially attached to the royal tombs – a system which had been in operation for 200 years by the time of Seti I. These craftsmen were the élite of their kind – everyone a master – and were treated as such. They lived with their families apart from the rest of the population in a walled village, of about seventy houses, some distance from the Valley at

Below Figure of the goddess Hathor, where a 'specialist' in yellow paint has carelessly painted over the finished detail of her eye. Tomb of Su-em-niwet: corridor, south wall.

Above Ceiling of the burial chamber of King Seti I, magnificently decorated in black and yellow paint, showing the twelve hours of the night and the heavenly constellations represented in various human and animal forms. Valley of the Kings. c.1280 BC.

Overleaf View, from the south, of the village of Deir el-Medina, which housed the community of artists who worked in the royal tombs in the Valley of the Kings. New Kingdom. c.1504–1099 BC.

a place called today Deir el-Medina. The ancient Egyptians called the village 'the Place of Truth' and the workmen 'servants in the Place of Truth'.

Fortunately for us, they were an unusually literate community and left behind copious records of their activities, especially from the periods of the Nineteenth and Twentieth Dynasties, written in hieratic sometimes on papyrus but more usually on bits of broken pottery or limestone called *ostraca*. We know from these that the workmen of a tomb were divided into two gangs, a right and a left, who probably worked the two sides of a tomb simultaneously, each in the charge of a foreman. There was also a 'scribe of the tomb', who kept a daily record of progress and a register of attendance. The normal number of workmen was about sixty, though this could vary as appropriate. They consisted of stonemasons, carpenters, sculptors, draughtsmen and painters. Posts in the workforce were generally hereditary, passing down from father to eldest son, sometimes over several generations. They worked an eight-hour day with a break in the middle and had a day off every ten days, though they were also entitled to special holidays on the occasions of festivals to the gods. The intitial hollowing out

Above Scene showing King Ramesses II in his chariot at the Battle of Qadesh, truimphantly leading his forces and slaying the Hittites. From the temple of Abu Simbel, c.1270 BC.

of a tomb appears never to have taken more than two years or so. Its decoration, on the other hand – the composition of the scenes, the relief sculpting, the painting – would have taken a great deal longer, which is why most of the tombs were unfinished at the king's death. Seti I's tomb is one of the few exceptions.

Money as we know it did not exist in ancient Egypt. The workmen's pay consisted of rations of grain, supplemented by supplies of fish, vegetables, wood for fuel, pottery and occasional treats of meat, wine and beer. Any surplus could be exchanged for other products, using a system of relative values

expressed in *deben*. There are many records of such transactions, involving payment for household and funerary furniture, livestock and luxury commodities, showing that this was an affluent community, something that is also evident from the size and quality of some of their own tombs.

Decline and Collapse

Two hundred years after Egypt's first imperial conquests, the records of Deir el-Medina and the splendour of tombs such as that of Seti I present a picture of continuing domestic prosperity. Abroad, however, dark clouds had long been gathering on Egypt's imperial horizons. Another great military power, the Hittite empire, based in Anatolia (now Turkey), had arisen in the north and now threatened Egypt's domination. The conflict came to a head during the reign of Seti I's son, Ramesses II (1279–1213 BC), when a great battle took place in 1274 BC between the two powers near a town called Qadesh in Syria.

Though widely celebrated on Egyptian temple walls as a great victory for Ramesses, the outcome was at best a draw. Ultimately Ramesses was obliged to relinquish a great deal of the northern territories and to sign a peace treaty with the Hittite king. The Egyptian empire in the Near East had been delivered a blow from which it was never fully to recover. The story thereafter is one of gradual decline, punctuated by periods of brief resurgence, with Ramesses' successors fighting a series of rearguard actions against a variety of hostile forces coming from different directions. Within a century or so of his death the empire had completely gone.

During the same period, significantly, the supply of Nubian gold appears to have diminished. The routes to the desert mines were more difficult to traverse, owing probably to the increased aridity already evidenced in the drying up of the Nile channels in the Dongola Reach (see pages 128–9). Records appear to indicate that under the last great pharaoh of the New Kingdom, Ramesses III (1184–1153 BC), second king of the Twentieth Dynasty, only a few *deben* of gold were dedicated annually to the temple of Karnak, a paltry amount when compared to the vast sums donated by his predecessors at the height of the empire.

From the same king's reign we have further evidence of economic decline. An official document records that payment to the Deir el-Medina workmen was delayed for a period of six months resulting in them marching in protest, demonstrating and withdrawing their labour on the king's tomb – the first recorded strike in history. The same document states that a number of workmen were charged with attempting to enter illegally a number of royal tombs with a view to plundering them. They were caught before any harm was done, but others were later to succeed, as is clearly shown by the transcript of a court case during the reign of Ramesses IX (1126–1108 BC) recording the testimony of a stonemason, Amenpnufer, who was charged with tomb-robbery and confessed after having been 'beaten with sticks' and having his 'feet and hands twisted':

> 'We went to rob the tombs in accordance with our regular habit, and we found the pyramid tomb of King Sekhemreshedtawy, Son of Ra, Sobekemsaf, this being not at all like the pyramids and tombs of the nobles which we habitually went to rob. We took our metal tools and forced a way into the pyramid of this king through its innermost part. We found its underground chambers, and we took lighted candles in our hands and went down. Then we broke through the rubble...and found this god lying at the back of his burial-place. And we found the burial-place of Queen Nubkhaas, his queen, situated beside him...We opened their sarcophagi and their coffins...and found the noble mummy of this king...We collected the gold we found on the noble mummy of this god together with that on his amulets and jewels...We collected all that we found upon her likewise and set fire to their coffins...Thus I, together with the other thieves who are with me, have continued down to this day in the practice of robbing the tombs of the nobles and people of the land who rest in the west of Thebes. And a large number of people of the land rob them as well, and are as good as partners of ours.'

Amenpnufer and his gang were found guilty and would have suffered, in penalty, the cruellest of deaths, impaling on a stake. But despite the severe penalties, sporadic tomb-robbery continued, encouraged by administrative corruption and laxity, as the Twentieth Dynasty drew to a close in the midst of economic and political turmoil. Central authority collapsed and the country split into two, into a northern and southern kingdom, each under its own ruler. The southern kingdom fell under the effective control of the High Priest of Amun–Ra in the temple of Karnak, who had become an enormously powerful figure, more powerful than the king himself. The last king of the Dynasty, Ramesses XI (1099–1069 BC), had begun a tomb in the Valley of the Kings but, fearing for its ultimate safety, had left it unfinished and moved elsewhere in the country. After 400 years of continuous occupation, the community of workmen abandoned Deir el-Medina, never to return. No royal tomb would ever again be built in the Valley of the Kings.

Crisis followed crisis, as the Viceroy of Kush, a man called Panehsy, rebelled successfully against the authority of the southern kingdom. Nubia became independent again and the gold mines were lost. Egypt's Age of Gold had truly come to an end.

These events sealed the fate of the royal tombs. Full of gold bullion and other precious commodities, they offered an irresistible temptation, and not just to tomb-robbers. The Egyptologist Dr Nicholas Reeves has recently suggested that the greatest threat came from the State itself. While campaigning against Panehsy in Nubia, the High Priest and General Piankh wrote a letter to a senior official in Thebes ordering him to 'uncover a tomb amongst the tombs of the ancestors and preserve its seal until I return'. The implications seem clear: in these times of need, it had become official practice to enter sealed tombs and recycle their contents for the State's purposes, in the case of Piankh probably to fund the war against Panehsy.

With the security and integrity of the necropolis so compromised, the policy was adopted of removing the royal mummies from their original tombs, rewrapping them where necessary, and reinterring them in new locations. Eventually two secret caches were created, in reused tombs, one inside and one outside the Valley. Here the mummies were reburied without any of their original burial equipment or precious accoutrements. The threat posed by tomb robbers was no doubt one reason for this policy of collective reinterment. But Reeves believes that in these straitened economic times the

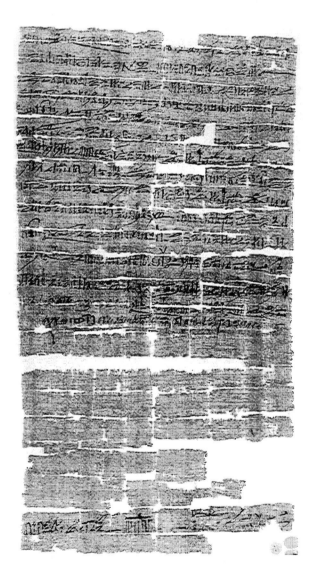

Right Letter in the hieratic script on papyrus to the High Priest and General Piankh from necropolis officials, confirming that they have carried out his instructions to 'uncover a tomb amongst the tombs of the ancestors and preserve its seal until I return' – an indication, scholars now believe, that it had become official policy to enter the royal tombs in the Valley of the Kings and strip them of their valuables for the use of the State. From Thebes, Twentieth Dynasty. c.1071 BC.

situation suited the authorities very well, providing a convenient pretext for
entering the tombs, removing the owners and systematically appropriating
whatever gold and other treasure lay within. Only Tutankhamun escaped –
the location of his tiny tomb no doubt long forgotten – to give us a tantaliz-
ing glimpse of what vast riches the tombs in the Valley of the Kings must
once have contained.

Whatever the motives, it is a policy for which we today should be enormously grateful. The secret caches remained hidden and undisturbed for

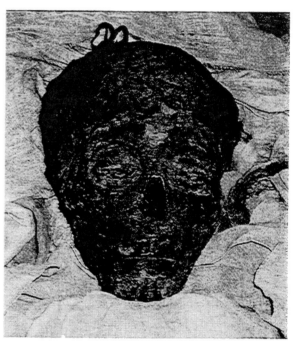

Left The burial chamber, the 'house of
gold', of King Tutankhamun, with its
stone sarcophagus and the king's outer
coffin, made of gilded wood, which
contains the royal mummy. Tutankhamun
was originally buried wearing a gold
mask within a nest of three coffins, the
innermost one made of solid gold. The
mask and the other two coffins are now
in the Cairo Museum. Thebes, Valley of
the Kings, Eighteenth Dynasty, c.1327 BC.

Above Head of the mummy
of King Ahmose (c.1525 BC).
From Thebes.

nearly three millennia until their discovery in the last decades of the nineteenth century. When examined, they were found to contain some seventy
bodies in total, including the mummies of most of the pharaohs of the New
Kingdom, over twenty in number, many still in very good condition. As a
result, we can gaze at the actual faces of some of the greatest names of the
Age of Gold: of Ahmose and Thutmose I, who helped to create it, of Seti I
and Ramesses II, who fought to maintain it, and of Ramesses III and his successors, under whom it fell into final decline.

DEITIES AND DEMONS

The images on the tomb walls of the ancient Egyptians portray an idyllic existence along the banks of the Nile, but in truth it was also a life full of uncertainty. To understand and manage their world, the Egyptians populated it with an ever-growing array of divine beings – deities and demons who exercised influence on every aspect of life in this world and the next, and who had to be appeased, controlled and sometimes threatened.

Hathor, the great cow deity and mother of pharaoh, was the goddess of fertility and love; but when angered she could also destroy humanity. Sekhmet, the lioness, symbolized the nurturing warmth of the sun, but she also evoked its scorching heat and deadly pestilence. Selket, the scorpion, could give or take breath away; her sting gave her the power to grant life or death. Khnum, a ram-headed god, brought forth the life-giving waters of the Nile flood, yet he could also hold it back.

The appearance of the gods stemmed from the observation of nature. Certain creatures were perceived to embody special qualities – strength in the lion, virility in the ram, speed and sight in the falcon. The dualistic qualities of the gods derived from the experience of life: the universe had its good side and its bad and it had to be constantly kept in balance. To maintain this delicate equilibrium, which the Egyptians called *ma'at*, they needed to ensure the benevolence of the gods who made up their universe – gods born at the beginning of time and created with creation.

Below The scorpion goddess Selket, a guardian of the living and the dead. Bronze. Late Period, after 600 BC.

Right Sekhmet, the lady of life, was a lioness personifying the warmth of the sun, but she could also scorch and burn. Grano-diorite. Reign of Amenhotep III (c.1390-1352 BC).

Above The great snake of the underworld. Apep, symbolized the primeval forces of chaos. Described as over 16 m (52 ft) long, his front part made of flint, he tried to capsize, ground and swallow the sun boat as it passed through the night. Tomb of Seti I (c.1294–1279 BC), Valley of the Kings.

Above Apep was so dangerous that even his name had to be magically killed. Here a knife severs the neck of the hieroglyphic determinative of his name. Tomb of Seti I, Valley of the Kings.

To the Egyptians, creation was not a single, isolated event but an ongoing cycle of renewal to be repeated daily with the rising of the sun, as the sun god emerged anew from the mound of creation victorious over the demons of the netherworld who sought to destroy him each night. Chief among these demons and agents of chaos was the giant snake Apep, who tried to hinder the progress of the sun boat with the coils of his writhing body. Every god played a part in warding off Apep's attacks throughout the night and ensuring creation each morning. Only by constant and correct obser-

Above The massive ceremonial gateways, called pylons, at the front of each temple, represented the mouains of the horizon. Mortuary Temple of Ramesses III (c.1184–1153 BC) at Medinet Habu.

vance of their cults could the creative cycle be guaranteed and the forces of chaos kept at bay.

The cult of the gods took place in temples that were carefully designed to mirror the cosmos at that first perfect moment of creation, and the rituals that took place within them were a metaphor of the process of creation itself. At the height of Egypt's greatness in the New Kingdom (1550–1069 BC), temples were built to embody creation on a grand scale. At the front of each temple stood a soaring monumental gateway, called a pylon. Aligned so that

Opposite The closed bud on this lotus plant column suggests the fertile potential of creation about to unfurl within the inner sanctum of the temple. Mortuary Temple of Ramesses III at Medinet Habu.

the sun rose or set between its twin towers, it represented the horizon. On each tower scenes of pharaoh overwhelming his enemies served as powerful sentinels, conferring protection against the imperfection and threats of the exterior world. Each morning just before dawn, priests, ritually purified, shaven of all hair and clad only in the purest linen, entered through this gate into the festival courtyard, open to the sky, decorated with the kings' exploits undertaken on the god's behalf. From here, as the floor level rose and the ceilings became lower, the priests travelled from the outermost edges of the ordered world to the inner core of creation – the mound.

One ramp led up to a semi-lit hall filled with columns shaped like the papyrus and lotus plants which grew in the primeval marsh surrounding the

Right In a shrine of the hardest stone, the image of the god rested in his sanctuary in the darkness of pre-existence until the daily rituals roused him. Temple of Edfu. Graeco–Roman Period.

rising mound. Then another took them into the inner sanctum and the pitch blackness of the holy of holies, the pinnacle of creation. Here in his shrine the deity rested in his cult statue in the pure silence and darkness of pre-existence. Breaking the seal on the door to this sanctuary, the priests entered the holy place chanting prayers and burning incense. As the sun rose the god was roused and the cosmos was reborn.

On the temple walls, every need of the god was shown attended to by the king. It was the king who bathed, adorned, and anointed the statue of the god. It was the king, too, who laid out sumptuous feasts for the god's nourishment. In reality a cadre of priests enacted the rituals in the name of their master, declaring to the god, 'It is the king who sends me'. This was not a matter of self-aggrandizement on the part of the king, but a necessary part of the mainte-nance of the Egyptian world. The king was the representative of mankind. Offering the fruits of the earth to the god enabled the god to reciprocate by offering important things back to the king, such as years of eternity upon the throne, stability in government, strength and success. In this fashion the offer-ings would reconfirm the creation of the world as the Egyptians knew it.

Unlike a modern house of worship, Egyptian temples functioned more like machines engineered to keep the cycle of the universe in motion. This was a technical operation that required a qualified staff and specialized knowledge, thereby excluding the majority of the population, in order to ensure that the crucial task of survival was never impaired. The fact that the people couldn't go in, however, did not mean that the god couldn't come out.

Oracles

The Egyptians put their faith in what at first glance appears to be a baffling number of divine beings. Although not all had temples, there were gods of the physical world, including the earth and sky; gods who embodied abstract ele-ments such as wisdom and love; and gods of specific locations. Throughout history every town and village in Egypt had a local deity. If the town produced a line of pharaohs, the prominence of that local god rose. And so it was in Thebes: beginning with the New Kingdom around 1550 BC, the local god Amun united with the sun god Ra to reign as the king of the gods, just as the princes of Thebes now reigned as kings of Egypt. The cult statue of Amun–Ra resided in the main temple of the state, the magnificent temple at Karnak, the largest temple ever built. Yet, like everyone, he enjoyed getting out now and again to visit the other temples and shrines that filled ancient Thebes.

Left The king, as representative of all mankind, is shown tending to every need of the god, here Ra–Harakhty, to ensure the smooth running of the universe. Temple of Ramesses II (1279–1213 BC). Abu Simbel.

Overleaf The temple of Karnak at Thebes, mansion of the state god Amun–Ra. In the foreground is the sacred lake in which the priests purified themselves.

Above Amun–Ra came out on festival days in his travelling boat, carried on the shoulders of priests. Too sacred and powerful an image to be viewed directly, his statue is hidden by a curtain. From Karnak, the Red Chapel of Hatshepsut (c. 1479–1457 BC).

For the majority of the population the most direct encounter with this great god of state occurred when his cult statue came out of its sanctuary on the occasion of major festivals. The most important of these was the 'beautiful feast of Opet', when the statues of Amun, his wife Mut and their son Khonsu were escorted in a great and joyous procession down an avenue of sphinxes, 2 miles (3.2 km) long, to the temple of Luxor to relive their honeymoon.

It was an event eagerly anticipated. A riot of activity erupted when they appeared at the door of the temple in their ceremonial travelling barques hoisted on to the shoulders of priests. Soldiers and citizens chanted hymns of praise, others kneeled in adoration and kissed the ground. Musicians,

Nubian dancers and acrobats performed for the gods, priests clapped their hands and women shook rattles. Along the route specially built chapels filled with offerings provided rest stops for the god and the priests, while vendors lined the way supplying food to the masses.

Such occasions also provided the opportunity to ask the god for his judgement, for an oracle. As the procession drew near, a petitioner would dash in front of the barque and beg a consultation. If the god agreed, the procession halted to hear a yes or no question posed to the god: 'Will an unpopular foreman be removed from the job? Will a loved one return from a journey safely? Should I buy this cow? Are these things true?' A step forward meant yes, a step back no.

If the reply was unsatisfactory, it was possible to consult another oracle or even ask the same god again on another occasion. A papyrus in the British Museum records the remarkable case of Petjau-em-di-amun who was picked out by the oracle as a thief responsible for stealing five tunics. Denying the allegation, he took his own case to another oracle which confirmed the verdict. After appealing unsuccessfully two more times, he finally, after a certain amount of physical inducement, confessed his guilt. Following an additional one hundred lashes of the cane, he also promised not to retract his confession. Interestingly, it still remains unclear whether the garments were ever recovered.

The use of oracles was not confined to the ordinary populace. They were also consulted by kings, when divine approval or ratification was required for some extraordinary decision, course of action or series of events. Nothing could have been more extraordinary, in terms of the Egyptians' view of the correct order of things, than the ascension to the throne of Queen Hatshepsut following the death of her husband, Thutmose II, in 1479 BC. Since the legitimate successor, Thutmose III (his son by another queen), was too young to rule in practice, it was arranged that his step-mother Hatshepsut should act as regent during the boy king's minority. Within two years, however, she had assumed the throne herself and been crowned as king, a position she occupied for twenty years. During this period, Thutmose III was officially co-ruler but was very much the subordinate partner. Whether this course of events arose out of personal ambition, as has traditionally been thought, or (more likely) was dictated, at least initially, by some political necessity, is uncertain. But one thing is clear: a female on the throne of Egypt ran contrary to *ma'at*. Horus, the king, had always to be a man.

Sanction for such a drastic departure could only come from Amun–Ra, the king of the gods, and it was here that the device of the divine oracle was invoked. In an inscription carved on her famous 'Red Chapel' at Karnak, the official line was promoted that, during a festival procession in the temple of Luxor, Amun–Ra had prophesied Hatshepsut's ascent to the throne through 'a very great oracle…proclaiming for me the kingship of the Two Lands, Upper and Lower Egypt'. A series of scenes in the same chapel actually depicts Amun–Ra crowning her as king – an iconographic programme designed to confirm her legitimacy. After an initial period when she had been represented as a woman, she is now consistently shown dressed as a king with the body of a man (though interestingly the texts accompanying the scenes persist in some-

Above As the oracle ordained. Hatshepsut, depicted with the body of a man, is crowned king by Amun–Ra, with the goddess Hathor in attendance. The Red Chapel. Karnak.

times referring to her as a female). The special sanction was not, however, to last much beyond her reign. The strength of centuries of convention was too great, and the Hatshepsut episode was so fundamentally at variance with *ma'at* that its record could not be allowed to survive. In due course, her image and cartouches as king were systematically erased or removed from view.

It is unlikely that common folks could approach Amun–Ra during such an important time as the Opet Festival. There were numerous lesser shrines

Right The queen who would be king: statue of Hatshepsut, shown in her more feminine guise from early in her reign, yet still in the full regalia of kingship. From Thebes, Deir el-Bahri.

whose deities could be consulted. Nevertheless, new evidence indicates that the great gods of Thebes came out more often than previously thought. In fact, it now emerges that Amun–Ra left his house every ten days; his destination was a little temple across the river, whose small size belies its importance.

Medinet Habu

In the northeast corner of the huge enclosure surrounding the mortuary temple of Ramesses III, called today Medinet Habu, stands a small temple which was already old when Ramesses was born. Long after his sprawling temple had fallen into disuse, this temple continued to attract the attention of kings who restored it and added to it for over 1500 years. Since 1994 a

Above Peter Dorman records the reliefs in the sanctuary of the 'genuine mound of the west', the home of the primeval gods of creation. Hatshepsut Temple at Medinet Habu.

team of Egyptologists from the University of Chicago's Oriental Institute has been restoring and recording its fine inscriptions and reliefs, and working to unlock the secret of its holiness and its history.

Probably a sacred site since the Middle Kingdom, its earliest surviving structure, the sanctuary, was built by Queen Hatshepsut. As Director Dr Peter Dorman explains:

'Like all monuments built by Hatshepsut, the temple exhibits extensive recarving, renovation and repainting. Hatshepsut suffered a posthumous historic revision at the hands of her stepson

Thutmose III, and her names throughout were altered. In other places her figure was entirely effaced and replaced by a fully laden table of offerings. However, through the layers of later paint and plaster, traces of her original figure may be seen to varying degrees, often accompanied by devotional inscriptions.'

The significance of the temple can be determined from several inscriptions. To the Thebans, it marked the spot where the original mound of creation came into being. Proclaimed 'the genuine mound of the west' and called 'the mound of the fathers and mothers', it was the home of the eight primeval gods who, according to one myth, existed before creation and came together to form the creation mound. Called the Ogdoad or 'Group of Eight', they were four pairs of male and female deities representing the primordial elements, one of whom was Amun, the god of hidden power.

But why here? The edge of the desert seems an odd location for a mound

Médinet Habu

Desert   Nile   Desert

Above Cross-section of the Nile Valley at Thebes. Because the flood plain is higher than the low desert which surrounds it, before the Nile overflowed its banks the rise in the water-table was evident in the desert margins. *(After Marc Gabolde)*

Right The side entrance to the genuine mound of the west Hatshepsut Temple at Medinet Habu.

Above The well-preserved remains of some of the houses in the famous village of the royal tomb-builders at Deir el-Medina.

arising out of the water, but new research on the geomorphology of the Nile Valley makes it in fact the natural place. With each inundation the Nile deposited a layer of silt on its banks, and over the millennia this silt has built up to make the flood-plain higher than the low desert which surrounds it. Long before the Nile would have actually flooded its banks each year, a rise in ground water would be noticed in the low desert, particularly where the high plateau of the desert was close by. The water and marsh plants which surrounded the temple before the flood, and probably for a while thereafter, gave it its visible and long-lasting sanctity.

Amun–Ra came to this spot to commune with his brethren every ten days, or once a week according to the Egyptian calendar. This must have provided

ample opportunities for oracles from even this great god. But for day-to-day life, the gods and their power could be found closer to home.

Deir el-Medina

Deir el-Medina, as it is now called, was the home of the craftsmen who built the kings' tombs in the Valley of the Kings (see pages 142–7). Hidden away in the desert on the west bank of Thebes, both to protect the craftsmen's intimate knowledge of the royal tombs and to provide easy access to work, the dry environment has preserved it well.

Today, the outlines of seventy houses can still be counted, arranged to either side of a central path. Housing was provided by the state and was fairly standard in plan, although over the years individual touches were added. Despite certain variations in size and the number of rooms according to the status of the occupant, the typical house consisted of an antechamber or front room and a living-room characterized by a brick couch. Off that were two smaller rooms, possibly a bedroom and a kitchen. Conditions must have been cramped, but with food, water and even laundresses provided by the state, the lives of these skilled and literate craftsmen were probably not uncomfortable. Just beyond the town walls to the west, the craftsmen turned their skills to the construction and decoration of their own tombs, dug into the rock and topped with little pyramid-shaped chapels. When royal tomb-building ceased at the end of the Twentieth Dynasty the workers and their families stayed on, but marauding nomads soon forced them to abandon their village rapidly, never to return, leaving behind personal possessions, and most importantly, written documents. Uniquely preserved, Deir el-Medina, more than any other place in Egypt, has provided a glimpse into the everyday lives of the ancient Egyptians – lives which were touched by deities and demons from the cradle to the grave and beyond.

Birth

The greatest threat to life came at birth. The day of birth was a day of joy, but like the creation of the world itself, it too was fraught with peril. It was a dangerous interface of life and death, when demons conspired to cause harm and deities had to use all their protective powers to prevent it. As was the case until quite recently, the mortality rate at birth for both mother and child was high; a special cemetery at Deir el-Medina for infants and young children contained over a hundred graves.

To prevent the demons who were massing from overrunning the house, on the day of delivery the mother-to-be retired to a special place. Here mother and child would remain in seclusion for about two weeks after the birth, during which time attendants looked after them, adorning the mother, purifying her, making her ready to rejoin the community as a vibrant and healthy new mother. In the more spacious surroundings of rural farmsteads or the villas of city officials, birth took place in an airy tent-like pavilion hung with vines and festive bowers erected in the garden, but in the crowded village of Deir el-Medina, an enclosed platform in the front room of the house may have served this purpose.

Found in almost half of all the houses at Deir el-Medina, this structure is called a 'birth-box'. It was a rectangular construction of mud brick, partially or fully enclosed, except for an opening on its long side, which was approached by set of steps and was originally plastered and painted with the bizarre images of two powerful deities, the god Bes and the goddess Tawaret.

Bes was a bandy-legged dwarf with the mane and tail of a lion, his tongue protruding over sharp teeth in a gesture meant to intimidate enemies. Bes is actually a convenient name for nearly a dozen different gods, all represented in almost identical ways. He could be Aha, the fighter, or Hayet or Tetetenu, all of whom safeguarded women in labour and young children. His images on headrests, beds, furniture legs and mirrors served to keep demons away throughout the house, and as an amulet worn around the neck his frightening likeness provided constant protection.

Above An *ostracon* shows a healthy new mother with her hair specially dressed, clad in jewels and special sandals, enjoying the festivities as she rejoins the community after her period of seclusion. From Deir el-Medina. New Kingdom, c.1300–1100 BC.

Right An enclosed raised platform in the front room of a house at Deir el-Medina may have served as a 'birth box'.

Opposite above Tawaret was a powerful protectress of women in childbirth. From Deir el-Medina. Nineteenth Dynasty.

Opposite below Squatting on bricks in the 'birth box', a woman gives birth with the support of Hathor, the cow-headed goddess of love and fertility. Relief from the Temple of Hathor at Dendara, now in Cairo Museum. Graeco–Roman Period.

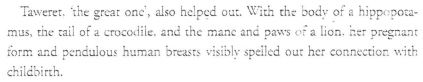

Taweret, 'the great one', also helped out. With the body of a hippopotamus, the tail of a crocodile, and the mane and paws of a lion, her pregnant form and pendulous human breasts visibly spelled out her connection with childbirth.

As the birth drew near, the labouring woman kneeled or squatted on special 'birth bricks' attended by midwives representing the goddess Isis, the epitome of the good mother, and her sister Nephthys. The goddess Hathor, the great cow goddess of love, fertility and birth, was also invited to attend – not surprisingly, she was one of the most important deities in ancient Egypt. From her great udder she nourished the kings of Egypt, and amulets from her sanctuary could prevent prolonged labour. Meanwhile, practitioners of the sacred arts, equipped with magical spells, amulets and medical prescriptions, were called in to perform special incantations and dances, invoking the gods to ensure a safe and speedy delivery.

A short distance from Deir el-Medina, but separated from it by 500 years, was a tomb apparently belonging to one of these practitioners in the late Middle Kingdom. The tomb shaft, found below a much later storeroom of the Ramesseum, the mortuary temple of

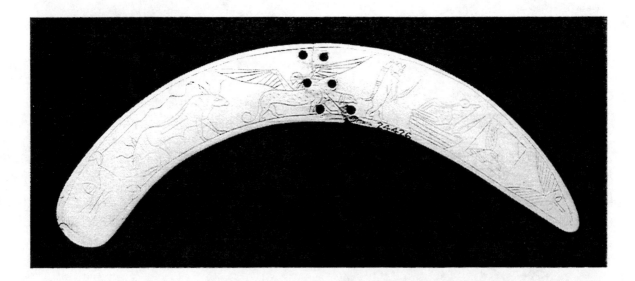

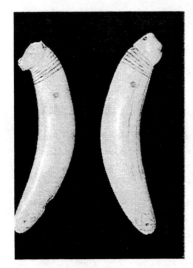

Top Magical knife for protecting mother and child. Hippopotamus ivory, c. 1800 BC.

Above A pair of ivory clappers for frightening away demons. From Lahun in the Fayum, c. 1900–1750 BC.

Right By donning this (much used) painted-canvas mask, an attendant channelled the power of Beset during the delivery rites for mother and child. From Lahun in the Fayum, c. 1900–1750 BC.

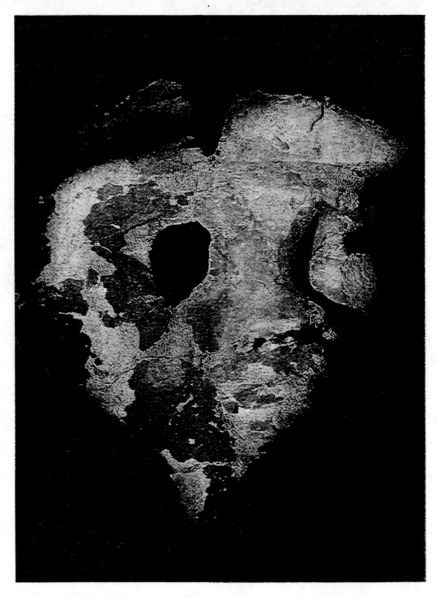

Ramesses II, led to a much disturbed burial chamber, but within it was a wooden box containing his remarkable kit.

The box contained twenty-three fragmentary papyrus rolls, a bundle of reed pens, and a unique collection of amulets, figurines and implements that were used to protect mother and child. There were ivory clappers in the shape of hands to frighten away evil spirits, female figurines to ensure the mother's safety and continued fertility, and a set of four magical wands or apotropaic (i.e. evil-averting) knives, made from hippopotamus tusk. These were used to draw a circle of protection around the mother-to-be and later, the sleeping child. Too powerful to be placed in the grave intact, they were broken in antiquity, but show evidence of extensive use. Inscribed on such wands are figures representing a mixture of malevolent and protective elements. To be effective, the child was identified with the young sun god Ra, who battles the forces of chaos. As Ra emerges victorious over his enemies to achieve his own birth each morning, so too, through the use of such a wand, would the child. At one tip is a canine head, a sign denoting the ancient Egyptian word for 'power'. The severed head of a donkey represents chaos defeated with the help of the gods: the frog goddess Heket, another goddess of childbirth; Tawaret, who wields her knife; and other composite deities.

Among the most extraordinary objects found in this kit were a wooden statuette of Beset, the female counterpart of Bes, holding a bronze snake staff in each hand just as she is often depicted on the knives, and an actual snake staff of bronze originally discovered entangled in a mass of hair to strengthen its personal effect. Although not found among the equipment in this box, in another contemporary but less extensive kit unearthed in the Fayum, a life-size and much-used mask transformed a priestess or attendant into a conduit for the divine and protective strength of Beset, just like the statuette, to empower the spells written on the papyrus rolls.

There was a spell 'to release a child from the belly of its mother', 'to make protection for a child on the day of its birth', tests to determine whether the baby would live or die, and other incantations to restore health to the mother herself.

Left This rare statuette of Beset acted as a conduit for her protective power. From Thebes, magician's kit, c. 1850–1750 BC.

But the Ramesseum practitioner dealt not just with birth. Other papyri in his box contained spells and prescriptions for treating muscular pain and diseases of the eye, as well as texts for funerary rituals and hymns in praise of the king. A 'knower of things', as the Egyptians called him, he was no itinerant magician. The decoration on the lid of his box identifies him as a *hery seshta*, 'one who is over the secrets', a title of a specific priestly rank within the state temples. And the magic that he used to assist in childbirth was no different from the magic that made the gods awake in their temples. Magic, or *heka*, was what made creation possible and carried none of the unsavoury connota-

Below The embodiments of perception, Sia, and magic, Heka, accompany the god Ra and help pilot his boat through the dangerous landscape of the underworld. Tomb of Seti I, Valley of the Kings.

tions it has acquired in modern times. Magic was what kept the universe going. Personified as a god, in the company of Sia (wisdom or perception) and Hu (divine pronouncement). Heka helped pilot the boat of the sun god Ra through the treacherous terrain of the underworld to achieve rebirth each morning.

Magic and Myth

Egyptian magic worked in a very specific way. First the problem had to be perceived and then the power or *heka* of the gods invoked. The Egyptians

maintained a belief that the perils of this life could be overcome through indentifying with the gods who overcame their own hardships. By far the most popular for assuaging personal afflictions were Osiris, Isis and Horus. The epic saga of their ordeals would form the basis of many Egyptian beliefs and practices.

When Ra wearied of ruling the earth, he retired to heaven, leaving his successors to reign in their turn. When Osiris attained kingship of the earth with his sister and wife Isis at his side, a golden age ensued, but it was not destined to last long. His brother Seth, jealous of his popularity, savagely murdered him, introducing death to the world. Isis revived him long enough to conceive a son, but despite her great powers, Osiris became the god of the dead.

Now alone in the world, Isis went into hiding in the marshes of the Delta, where she bore and raised her son, Horus, to avenge the murder of his father and reclaim his rightful throne. The marshes were full of the emissaries of Seth – venomous snakes and scorpions, and deadly disease – but Isis, a dedicated mother, used all of her power to protect Horus by learning their names. To know something's name was to understand its essence, and thus to have control over it. Isis's exemplary care for her child, combined with her magical skills, made her the ideal deity to be invoked for cures and protection.

Episodes in the intricate myth of Isis and Horus became the active force behind many spells and amulets. Small stone stelae which became popular around 700 BC show Horus as a child standing on crocodiles and holding snakes, scorpions and other dangerous animals in each hand as their master, now made immune from their poison by the power of Isis. These were powerful amulets and the Egyptians believed that water poured on them was endowed with healing powers over bites and stings for those who drank it.

One of the most popular and distinctive Egyptian amulets was the Wedjat or eye of Horus. The universal symbol of healing and wholeness, it represents the eye that Horus lost during the battle with Seth to avenge his father's murder. Luckily, the ibis-headed god of

Left Using his great wisdom, the ibis-headed god Thoth was able to restore the eye that Horus lost while avenging his father's death. Called a Wedjat, the eye became a universal symbol of health and wholeness as well as piety and self-sacrifice. Gold amuletic figurine, c.1000 BC.

Above left The hardships Isis endured to raise her son Horus made her the ideal mother whose immense curative powers were frequently invoked. Edfu Temple. Graeco-Roman Period.

wisdom, Thoth, was able to retrieve the eye, and as the moon waxed he slowly put it back together and restored it to health. In the same way, the Egyptians believed that injuries incurred without blame could be cured with the wisdom and the power of the divine.

Based on years of observation and experience, the Egyptians had also developed a body of medical knowledge, which they did not distinguish clearly from magic. Medical care followed the same three basic steps that made magic effective: observation of the patient's condition; diagnosis of the problem; and active treatment which could take the form of a prescription of herbs, a medical procedure or an incantation or spell.

When illness struck, the Egyptians called in a priest or physician, often one and the same, who consulted medical papyri, his reference manuals for treatment. One literate inhabitant of Deir el-Medina named Kenherkhopeshef, however, had his own set of texts in his exceptionally extensive library and preferred to take care of himself. One of his self-treatments survives. Troubled by a particularly nasty headache, he wrote the following spell on a piece of papyrus to expel the demon responsible for it:

> 'Turn back Sahekek, demon which came forth from heaven and earth, whose eyes are in his head and whose tongue is in his buttocks. He feeds on excrement...he lives on dung...I know the name of your mother, I know the name of your father. I am the two hands of the headrest. Stay away from me.'

Complete with the instructions that the word be recited four times over arrows made of flax stems, the wear patterns on the papyrus suggest that it was then folded up and placed as a pillow on his headrest, which also survives.

Below The demon Sahekek is depicted as a nude child in the pose of someone with a very bad headache. He was said to originate from the far ends of Nubia. Ostracon, New Kingdom, thirteenth century BC. *(After Gardiner and Černy)*

Right Headrest of the scribe Kenherkhopshef, decorated with figures of various protective deities, among them the god Bes, who warded off evil demons from the headrest's owner as he slept. Limestone, Nineteenth Dynasty, thirteenth century BC.

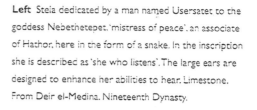

Left Stela dedicated by a man named Usersatet to the goddess Nebethetepet, 'mistress of peace', an associate of Hathor, here in the form of a snake. In the inscription she is described as 'she who listens'. The large ears are designed to enhance her abilities to hear. Limestone. From Deir el-Medina. Nineteenth Dynasty.

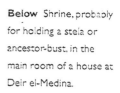

Below Shrine, probably for holding a stela or ancestor-bust, in the main room of a house at Deir el-Medina.

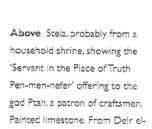

Above Stela, probably from a household shrine, showing the 'Servant in the Place of Truth Pen-men-nefer' offering to the god Ptah, a patron of craftsmen. Painted limestone. From Deir el-Medina. Nineteenth Dynasty.

The cause of an illness or adversity was not always clear. Perhaps the gods had been offended, or demons let loose. To keep the balance in their life, like the balance of the universe, the craftsmen at Deir el-Medina worshipped the gods. Around the exterior of the village were small chapels to gods and goddesses, places for group ritual observances with the workmen themselves serving as priests. But in the main living room of each house there was also a shrine, with a stela either set into the wall or placed on a pedestal, to the gods of their choice. Especially favoured, for obvious reasons, were Ptah, the patron god of craftsmen; Thoth, the god of writing; and the deified king Amenhotep I and his wife, founders of the village. The gods could be vengeful but forgiving. One stela reads, 'I am a man who swore falsely by Ptah and he made me go blind…He caused me to be like a dog in the streets, I being a man who had sinned against his Lord. Righteous was Ptah toward me, when he taught me a lesson. Be merciful to me, look on me in mercy!'

They also worshipped a goddess of more local significance. Poisonous snakes were common in their desert home, and one way to protect themselves from this danger was to venerate snake-deities. One of them, Meretseger, 'She who loves Silence', was to become a popular patron of the village, for in the Egyptians' dualistic view of the world, that which worked against you could also be cajoled to work on your behalf. Snakes made of clay placed at the doors of the house were also popular means for providing protection from deadly snakes as well as frightening nightmares.

This is an idea which has a long history; even the humble tombs of the people who built the pyramids at Giza invoked the destructive powers of dangerous creatures to protect them from intruders. On a false door recently discovered in this cemetery, its owner threatens: 'If anyone will disturb my tomb he will be eaten by a crocodile, a hippopotamus and a lion.' His wife threatens the same but adds snakes and scorpions to the list.

Ancestors

The dead could also be powerful allies. Because the afterlife was the realm of both deities and demons, the villagers at Deir el-Medina set up household shrines in their living-rooms where offerings were made to the busts and stelae portraying their ancestors. Now equipped with divine powers themselves, the dead had direct access to the gods and could intervene on behalf of their respectful family.

To communicate with them the Egyptians wrote 'letters to the dead' on papyrus and on the interior of bowls once heaped with offerings. These messages covered everything from legal problems to domestic strife and even chatty greetings. Couched in the form of a reciprocal agreement, one son implored his deceased father to exert some influence on the outcome of a court case, supply him with a healthy new son, and punish some maid-servants, possibly also deceased, who were currently annoying his wife. And while he was at it, another healthy child for his sister would also be welcome.

But not all ancestors were willing to intercede. Those who may have been slighted in death, or bore a grudge in life, could come back to haunt the family. In 1200 BC a man stalked by misfortune thought it might be the doing of his dead wife. To reproach her he wrote a letter reminding her that he'd been a caring husband, and it really wasn't his fault that he was away on business when she died. Whether she was guilty or not remains unknown. Identifying malevolent spirits and pernicious demons by name was a tricky business at best, but on the final journey into the afterlife, there was no room for error.

Below So-called 'ancestor-bust', the focus of a domestic cult at Deir el-Medina. The bust represented a recently deceased family member, who had attained a blessed state in the afterlife and was therefore well placed to act as a mediator between the family and the gods. Painted limestone. Nineteenth Dynasty.

Above Painted scene in the burial chamber of the 'Servant in the Place of Truth, Pashedu' at Deir el-Medina. The large seated figure is the god of the dead Osiris, his green skin symbolic of new growth and rebirth. The tomb-owner is shown behind him, as a small figure kneeling in adoration. Nineteenth Dynasty.

Overleaf The deceased and his wife pause before the gates of the underworld, which are guarded by an array of demons. Passage is possible only through knowledge and recitation of their secret names:'I know you, I know your name....' Book of the Dead of Ani, Nineteenth Dynasty.

The Dead

To become as one with Osiris, the god of the dead, and travel in the solar boat with Ra, entailed a dangerous journey. There were obstacles and traps to be negotiated, monsters and demons to be avoided or confronted. Doom and eternal damnation awaited the ignorant or unwary. For these reasons, the Egyptians developed a compilation of spells called the 'Spells for Going Forth by Day', now known as the 'Book of the Dead'.

A virtual guidebook to the afterlife, it was written on papyrus or linen and placed with the body to help the deceased recognize the inhabitants and landscape of the underworld so as to be able to pass through it unharmed. It was potent magic. Success was guaranteed: 'Whoever knows these texts is one who on the day of resurrection in the other world arises and enters in.'

The Book of the Dead contained spells for fetching a ferry-boat in the sky; for passing by the dangerous coils of Apep; for being transformed into any shape one might wish to take; and for guiding one through the proper responses in the hall of judgement.

But in order to attain bliss in the Egyptian version of heaven, the 'Field of

Left Head of a demon-figure, in the form of a hippopotamus with teeth bared, one of the inhabitants of the underworld and here an embodiment of disorder and danger. Wood coated with black resin. Probably from Thebes, Valley of the Kings, New Kingdom, c.1479–1108 BC.

Reeds', one had first to get past the demons who guarded its many gates. Each gate was a danger, a challenge, an obstacle, guarded by demons who would devour the souls of those destined for damnation. The key to disarming them was again to know their secret names: there was 'the barker', 'the raging one with hippopotamus face', 'he who devours filth from his hind parts', 'the unapproachable', 'the bloodsucker' and 'he whose eyes spew fire'. The deceased would approach each one and proclaim, 'I know you and I know your name.'

Dreams

The deceased were not the only visitors to the realm of the dead. At night sleepers could, through their dreams, enter the world beyond and commune with the gods. A dream was believed to be a revelation of truth, an omen of good or bad, though its meaning was not always clear. To help, people

Below Shabti-figure of the scribe Kenherkhopshef, one of the great 'personalities' of the community of royal workmen. From his tomb, as yet unidentified, at Deir el-Medina. Thirteenth century BC.

Right Figure of an underworld demon, facing frontwards, pulling at his beard, his legs curiously in profile. The unconventional pose and action evoke his chaotic nature. Wood coated with resin. From Thebes, Valley of the Kings. Twentieth Dynasty. c.1108 BC.

Above Section of the 'Book of Dreams', a unique composition, once part of the library of Kenherkhopshef. It contains a list of dreams, each one identified as 'good' or 'bad', with an explanation of their true meaning. Written in the hieratic script on papyrus. From Deir el-Medina. Nineteenth Dynasty, thirteenth century BC.

known to be gifted at interpreting dreams could be consulted, whether priests attached to temples or a local 'wise person' who had built up a reputation in the field. The scribe Kenherkhopshef of Deir el-Medina owned his own 'Book of Dreams', the only work of its kind to have survived to modern times, though one imagines there must have been others like it. It is a handy compendium listing many different types of dream, in each case with an explanation of how it was to be interpreted, though it must be said that some are rather vague and hedging, very much like modern horoscopes:

> 'If a man sees himself in a dream dead –
>   Good. It means a long life.'
> 'If a man sees himself in a dream, his bed catching fire –
>   Bad. It means driving away his wife.'
> 'If a man sees himself in a dream drinking warm beer –
>   Bad. It means suffering.'
> 'If a man sees himself in a dream looking out of a window –
>   Good. It means the gods hear his cries.'
> 'If a man sees himself falling off a wall –
>   Good. It means the issuing of a favourable edict.'
> 'If a man sees himself looking after monkeys –
>   Bad. It means change awaits.'

Kenherkhopshef himself was one of the great characters of Deir el-Medina, much mentioned in the records and not always to his credit. An assertive and self-confident man, he held the influential position of scribe of the workforce for over forty years during the Nineteenth Dynasty. Respected by his seniors, he was very unpopular with his subordinates for being autocratic, showing little appreciation of their work, and for abusing his position of power. Often absent from work, he was in the habit of removing men from their official duties in the royal tomb to carry out his own private commissions. He was twice indicted for bribery, though he got off on both occasions.

Though clearly a rogue, Kenherkhopshef appears nevertheless to have been an erudite man, and documents of his suggest that he had an interest in literature and history. We have no idea when or how he acquired the dream-book but it would have been an enormously valuable possession – to be used, no doubt, by himself and his family but also perhaps more widely. Given the importance attached to dreams and to their correct interpretation, possession of the compendium would surely have provided a commercial opportunity which someone of Kenherkhopshef's character would not have been slow to seize. On application, and for suitable recompense, he might well have been willing to make its contents available to the community at large.

When already well into his fifties, Kenherkhopshef married a girl, Naunakhte, over forty years his junior (she may have been as young as twelve at the time). The marriage was childless, and after his death most of his property, including the dream-book, passed to his wife. In due course, the book became the property of one of her sons by a second marriage, now a prized family heirloom, to which he proudly added his name.

Above John Ray at work transcribing a group of *ostraca* bearing texts in the demotic script, similar to those in the archive of Hor.

In the following centuries, dreams, as communicative and revelatory experiences, came to play an increasingly prominent role, at all levels of society, in the practice of people's religion and in the ordering of their lives. By the Ptolemaic period (305–30 BC), when Egypt was under Greek rule, dreams and their interpretation had become a lucrative industry, and dreaming a professional calling. People regularly paid specialists to interpret their dreams or even to dream for them.

One of the most successful of these dreamers was a priest called Hor, who worked at the great cemetery of sacred animals at Saqqara, near the ancient city of Memphis, during the reign of King Ptolemy VI (180–145 BC). We know a great deal about Hor, as he left behind an archive of documents, a collection of about sixty-five texts written in ink on *ostraca* (pot-sherds) in Egyptian demotic, the script (a cursive form of hieroglyphs) developed for

Above View of the inside of one of the ibis galleries at Saqqara. Dr Nick Fieller, an archaeological statistician, examines one of the pottery jars containing an ibis mummy.

day-to-day use during the later periods of Egyptian history. Originally stored in a small chapel attached to the burial catacombs of the sacred ibis, the archive was discovered by an expedition of the Egypt Exploration Society in the 1960s and early 1970s. It has since formed a major focus of study for John Ray of the University of Cambridge, one of the world's leading authorities on demotic texts. Ray's work has shown that the documents record various events in Hor's career over a period of about twenty years up to 147 BC.

Hor began his career in the service of the goddess Isis in his home town near Sebennytos in the Delta. We learn from one of the texts that his life changed dramatically one night, in October 166 BC, when he had two dreams. One of them was humorous, the other more serious. In the first he dreams that he's walking up the great avenue between the temples where he works. It is night and he's surrounded by tombs. In the middle of the avenue

he is confronted by a ghost, who throws him into a panic by asking, 'Have you brought the food for 60,000 ibises?' In the other dream, he is working in a labour-gang, unpleasant work for a man of his standing. The foreman of the gang comes up to him and pays money for him to be released. Hor goes back to his home town, but the people of the labour-gang chase after him. They catch up with him and won't let him go. Suddenly the foreman appears and says, 'I am not a foreman. I am a god. Do not worship anybody except me.' And Hor replies, 'I will never do that again.' The god in question was Thoth. These dreams marked a turning-point in Hor's life. As a result of them, he moved from the Delta to Saqqara to serve the cult of the ibis god, Thoth, in the sacred animal necropolis.

Hor would have found no difficulty in making the move, as he was already a celebrated sage. Two years previously he had made a telling intervention at a time of national crisis. In 168 BC Egypt had been invaded by the Seleucid king of Syria, Antiochos Epiphanes. At the moment of maximum danger, Hor, who was attached at the time to the Egyptian army, had an important dream. Hor was granted an audience with Ptolemy himself, and assured him that all would be well, as indeed it turned out to be. His reputation was made.

The Sacred Animal Necropolis

The sacred animal necropolis at Saqqara is a huge burial complex, in the form of a series of underground galleries, containing vast quantities of mummified animals – baboons, cats, cows, dogs, hawks and ibises, each animal identified with a certain god, who was the subject of a cult. During the late first millennium BC, it was a great place of pilgrimage, with temples and shrines to which people came from far afield to make offerings and to commune with the gods, principally by paying for an animal or bird of their choice to be mummified and deposited, often enclosed in a pot, in one of the galleries. For a price, Hor was available for consultation by such pilgrims. Seeking divine guidance on matters of personal concern, perhaps a medical problem or a course of future action, they would pay Hor to have the god Thoth appear in one of his dreams and impart advice to them, a practice known as incubation. Hor would request the god to appear by reciting a special 'dream-invocation'. The god was not always prompt. Sometimes Hor had to wait several days.

John Ray regards such practices as serving an important social need, akin in some ways to modern-day therapy. The sacred animal cults belonged to the world of 'the ordinary guy', for whom the great temples remained inaccessible: 'Here you had something much more human, much more personal. Here you had gods who were interested in the little man, who could actually help him to sort out his problems.'

The priests, however, did not always do right by their customers. In addition to the accounts of his dreams, Hor's archive also contains records of an administrative nature, which shed fascinating and sometimes unfavourable light on the management and day-to-day practice of the animal cults. One particularly interesting document records an investigation into a corruption scandal, which centred on financial irregularities and the swindling of pilgrims, the latter process apparently involving the depositing of empty jars

Above The central shrine in the temple complex of the sacred animal necropolis at Saqqara, where Hor worked as a priest and dreamer. Along the cliff-face on either side are the entrances to a number of subterranean galleries where the sacred animals were buried in their millions.

rather than ones filled with bird mummies, for which the pilgrims had paid. A commission of inspectors was formed, and eventually six men, 'servants of the ibis' and 'servants of the hawk', were arraigned and imprisoned. As a result, the commission ordered a complete review of the arrangements for the burial of the sacred birds.

That such skulduggery was taking place has been borne out by modern examination of the bird mummies, recently carried out by Dr Paul Nicholson of the University of Cardiff, who has been investigating anew the galleries and their contents for the Egypt Exploration Society. Among other things, he has been carefully tracing the processes involved in the nurturing and preparation of the birds before their final deposition. It is known that the ibises were bred on a nearby lake, and examination of their remains has shown that in life they were well fed and looked after. When required by a pilgrim, they were killed (probably by breaking of their necks) and cursorily mummified, sometimes being desiccated and dipped into bitumen, before being wrapped in linen bandages and then placed in a pottery container, closed with a saucer-shaped lid. They were finally taken to the galleries, where they were stacked in various side chambers. This was not done on a one-by-one basis. One of Hor's documents indicates that a mass burial was performed once a year, when with appropriate ceremony the galleries would be specially opened for the occasion and then resealed. The ibis cult must have been one of the most popular. It is estimated that the galleries once held over four million ibises.

Nicholson and his team have found that, in general, the ibis mummies do indeed contain ibises. The same does not, however, hold true for the hawk mummies. A good proportion of these turn out to be 'pseudo-hawk mummies', shaped on the outside to look like hawks, but inside containing neither a hawk nor any kind of whole bird. He describes these pseudo-mummies as being varied in content:

> 'Some include parts of birds of prey, the bulk being made up of packing, sticks, or other bones; others contain large rodents, such as the Egyptian giant musk shrew. Ibis bones were sometimes used to supplement or substitute for the birds of prey, and in one instance ibis mandibles were used longitudinally to make a kind of frame around which linen was wrapped to form the mummy shape.'

Above left Paul Nicholson examining the mummy of an ibis. Preparation of the bird for burial involved dipping the body into some black resinous matter before wrapping it in linen. It was then placed in a pottery jar for final deposition in the galleries.

Left Bird mummy, skilfully wrapped and shaped to look like a hawk. Some specimens, when unwrapped, have turned out to be 'pseudo-mummies', containing little or no hawk remains. Late Period, after 600 BC.

Nicholson believes the explanation for this rampant cheating in the case of the hawk mummies lies in the fact that, unlike ibises, birds of prey are very difficult to breed in captivity and would, therefore, have needed to be trapped for use in the cults. The inevitably limited supply of such birds meant that a single specimen might be shared out among several mummies, while sometimes a mummy had to be completely faked.

One animal cult at Saqqara stands out from the rest in terms of both its importance and its meaning. This was the cult of the dead Apis bull, the origins of which probably go back to the earliest dynasties. Regarded while alive as a manifestation of Ptah, the creator god of Memphis, there was only one Apis at any one time, selected on the basis of colouring and certain other markings. The bull had to be black with, among other features, a white diamond-shaped mark on its forehead. He lived in pampered luxury in a special stall in the precincts of the great temple of Ptah in Memphis, served by a special cadre of priests, solicitous to his every need. He was the source of oracles and prophecies, certain aspects of his behaviour being regarded as significant for these purposes, and, like the king, he had a special window, from which he made public appearances.

The death of the Apis was an occasion for great national mourning, the corpse being afforded many of the rituals appropriate to the passing of the king. It was fully embalmed and purified in a special complex, some of whose structures have been identified close to the temple of Ptah. Among the most prominent features are a number of beautiful stone beds decorated with leonine heads and legs and with spouts and containers at one end for the discharge and containment respectively of liquid. These are often thought to have been the actual platforms on which the bulls were eviscerated and embalmed, but recently Michael Jones, an archaeologist working for the American Research Center in Egypt, has come to a different conclusion. He believes that, because the platforms are made of alabaster (calcite), a stone associated in the Egyptian mind with cleanliness and purity, the actual 'dirty work' of mummification must have been carried out elsewhere. For him, these magnificent beds would have been used only for the ritual purification of the mummies:

'the priests would have brought the completed mummy on a wooden carrying frame, placed it on top of the bed and poured libations of water over it... The water would have flowed out through the spout at the end and collected in the basin, whose enormous size gives some idea of the quantity of liquid needed for the purification process. The water could not be allowed to run anywhere. Having flowed over the body of the god, it was powerfully charged.'

Below Bronze figure of an Apis bull, with the characteristic mark on its forehead. Late Period, after 600 BC.

Above Stone platform used for the purification of the Apis-bull mummies. The vessel to hold the discharged liquid is still in place. Memphis. Late Period, after 600 BC.

Duly embalmed, the bull's body was transported along the processional way which linked Memphis and Saqqara for burial in a large stone sarcophagus, set in a vast underground catacomb specially reserved for the Apis bulls and known as the Serapeum. Just like humans, they were buried with various accoutrements, among them little *shabti*-figures, some with bull's heads to serve them in the afterlife. In death the Apis was identified with the god of the dead Osiris, to become the unity known as Osorapis.

The growth of the sacred animal cults represents an extraordinary religious development, the causes of which have been much debated. John Ray and others believe that, since it gained strength during a period of increasing political decline, towards the end of pharaonic history, and reached its zenith during a period of foreign occupation, the development may perhaps be best explained as the response of a native culture – dominated by foreigners and threatened with loss of identity – seeking to emphasize what was fundamentally and peculiarly its own. The Egyptians might have lost their independence and their position in the world, but they still had their own culture, their own special demons and deities. This made them different. This made them Egyptian.

The Nobility and Gentry, Visiters and Inhabitants of BATH and its Vicinity, are respectfully informed, that

TWO EGYPTIAN
MUMMIES,
A MALE AND FEMALE,

In the highest State of Preservation, *with various other Relics*,

BROUGHT TO THIS COUNTRY BY

Mr. BELZONI,

The celebrated Traveller, are now open for Exhibition at

10, New Bond-Street.

The MUMMIES are of the first Class: the Inspection of them it is presumed must be highly satisfactory to every Person, as exhibiting two distinct Specimens; the Bandages of the Male having been entirely removed from the Body, which is perfect, while the mode of applying them is beautifully illustrated in the Envelope of the Female.

The CASES are covered with Hieroglyphics, enriched with Ornaments most elaborately executed; the Interiors containing the Histories of the Lives of their very ancient Occupiers, in Egyptian Characters, as fresh as when inscribed by the Hand of the Artist, after a Lapse of probably

THREE THOUSAND YEARS.

"Perchance that very Hand, now pinioned flat,
"Has hob-a-nob'd with Pharaoh glass to glass,
"Or dropp'd a halfpenny in Homer's hat,
"Or doff'd its own to let Queen Dido pass,
"Or held, by Solomon's own invitation,
"A torch at the great Temple's dedication."

AMONG THE OTHER RELICS WILL BE FOUND

A MUMMY OF THE IBIS,
THE SACRED BIRD OF EGYPT;

An Urn with Intestines from Elei; an Inscription on the far-famed Paper of Egypt (the Papyrus); a massive Fragment of Granite with Hieroglyphics from Memphis; a variety of Idols in Stone, Clay, and Wood, from the Tombs of the Kings in the Valley of Beban-el-Malook, and the Ruins at Carnac; Urns, Vessels of Libation, Bronzes, Coins, &c. &c.

N.B. A few EGYPTIAN and other ANTIQUITIES for SALE.

Admittance, One Shilling each.

☞ PURCHASERS WILL BE ALWAYS RE-ADMISSIBLE.

A DESCRIPTIVE ACCOUNT of this COLLECTION will be published in a few Days.

WOOD and CO. Printers of the Bath and Cheltenham Gazette, UNION-STREET, BATH.

1842

Left The public display of mummies was popular entertainment and caused excitement throughout Europe. Belzoni poster, 1842.

EM

Nothing about the ancient Egyptians has captured the modern imagination more than their preserved remains: mummies. There is something indescribably fascinating about peering into the face of a person who departed this earth several thousand years ago, and few things make the ancient Egyptians come more to life than their corporeal remains in death. This is not only because of the pathos their remnants may evoke, but because modern scientific examination of them is providing exciting new insights into the conditions under which they lived.

Mummification evolved from the concept of preserving the body as a receptacle for the vital life force which survived death. To the ancient Egyptians, the preservation of the body by desiccating with salts, anointing with resins and wrapping in bandages was an important factor in attaining and maintaining an afterlife. To modern-day Egyptologists and scientists, it is a godsend of preserved material.

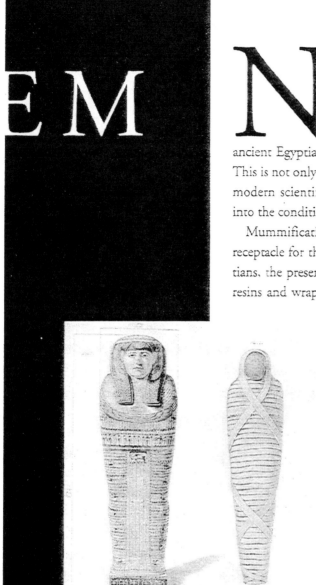

Above Following the opening up of Egypt after the Napoleanic expedition (1798–1801), mummies were exported in great numbers as 'curiosities'. Only later was their scientific significance appreciated. (*After Augustus Granville*)

Although we are all familiar with mummies, they have been an underestimated and ill-used resource. From medieval times well into the nineteenth century untold numbers of mummies were ground up for medicine. Their tissues, blackened by embalming oils, were believed to have the same medicinal powers as *mumia*, or bitumen, better known as asphalt, which was then found only in limited quantities in the Near East. The word 'mummy' comes from this use of the ancient bodies, but it now describes the body itself that has been either naturally or artificially preserved.

In the early nineteenth century, inspired by the discoveries that accompanied Napoleon's Nile campaign of 1798–1801, Egyptomania – the passion for anything Egyptian – swept Europe, and mummies became big business in a different way. To stock museums and the 'curiosity cabinets' of the well-to-do, a lucrative trade in Egyptian artefacts, including mummies, arose. The unwrapping of a mummy acquired on a young gentleman's tour of Egypt was an excuse for a fashionable soirée. Public exhibitions of mummies became popular sensations, and with the growth of tourism to Egypt, the desert hills were scoured for mummies to sell as *antikas*. There were plenty to find. The Italian adventurer Giovanni Belzoni, who made his fortune in the antiquities trade excavating monuments and tombs, recounts his exploration in the Theban hills: 'Every step I took I crushed a mummy in some place or another. Thus I proceeded from one cave to another, all full of mummies piled in various ways, some standing, some lying and some on their heads.'

Such discoveries led to a glut of mummies, and soon a more practical use was found for them. When faced with a severe shortage of rags for paper-making due to the American Civil War, an enterprising paper manufacturer in Maine named Isaac Augustus Stanwood had the idea of importing mummies from Egypt for their linen wrappings. Arriving by the boatload, the mummies were unwrapped and their bandages reduced to pulp in vats. The resins and oils used in the embalming process had stained the cloth, resulting in a heavy brown paper which proved to be especially suitable for meat wrapping. Stanwood was able to buy and ship tonnes of mummies for three cents a pound – less than half the price of buying rags at home. Reportedly covered in almost 30 lb of linen each, an entire mummy cost about a dollar. Stanwood would have continued this lucrative arrangement, had not a local outbreak of cholera, which included among its victims employees of Stanwood's paper-mill, brought it to a halt. Although the mummies were blamed for the epidemic, the tradition of brown paper in meat markets can still be found today.

But perhaps the most ignominious use of Egypt's legacy was as firewood. Mark Twain, in his humorous travel tale *The Innocents Abroad*, recounts seeing a railway engineer who, while stoking the furnace of a steam train with the shrivelled remains of the ancient Egyptians, exclaimed, 'Damn these plebeians, they don't burn worth a cent! Pass out a king!'

After surviving thousands of years, just how many mummies were lost during this episode is impossible to determine. Luckily, by the early nineteenth century the scientific potential of mummies had begun to be realized. In 1825 the young British physician Augustus Granville performed a scientific autopsy on the mummy of a woman named Irtyersenu, and published the results. He was able to determine that the woman had died in her fifties, had borne children, had a disease of the scalp and an ovarian cyst, but due to his careful storage of her remnants we now know that she probably died of pneumonia. It soon became clear how much could be learned from mummies.

Radiography

The invention of radiography (X-rays) in the 1890s marked an important new stage in the investigation of mummies. Unwrapping a mummy, even in a laboratory for the best scientific reasons, is an act of destruction. Henceforth, mummies could be examined non-invasively and their integrity preserved. However, while the potential of the technique was quickly realized, its application to mummies remained sporadic until the 1960s, since when its use has become standard. Mummies in museum collections are still unwrapped, but generally these days only in appropriate cases, for example when the condition of a mummy is known to be deteriorating.

Radiography allows an enormous amount of useful information to be gathered non-destructively. It reveals whether there is actually a body inside the wrappings, its sex, whether it suffered from injuries or certain diseases, and the likely age at death. It can also tell us a great deal about the techniques of mummification, but it has always had one major limitation. In a conventional X-ray plate, all of the internal features are superimposed, sometimes making their interpretation very difficult. Fortunately, in recent years a new enhanced form of radiography, making use of advanced computer technology, has been developed, which has no such limitation. This is the technique of computerized axial tomography, in short 'CAT-scanning' or 'CT-scanning'.

The value of CT-scanning in the examination of Egyptian mummies has been demonstrated by a number of collaborative projects carried out between the British Museum and various medical research departments in London hospitals. One of these projects involved the mummy of a 'chantress of Amun' who lived during the Twenty-second Dynasty (about 900 BC) named Tjentmutengebtiu. The mummy was examined in 1991–2 at St Thomas's Hospital, using a programme developed by Dr Stephen Hughes, Senior Medical Physicist. The Museum was represented by Dr John Taylor.

Below The intricately decorated case enveloping the mummy of Tjentmutengebtiu is made of cartonnage, a delicate material consisting of linen or papyrus stiffened with plaster. Direct examination of the mummy would entail destruction of the case. Twenty-second Dynasty, c. 900 BC.

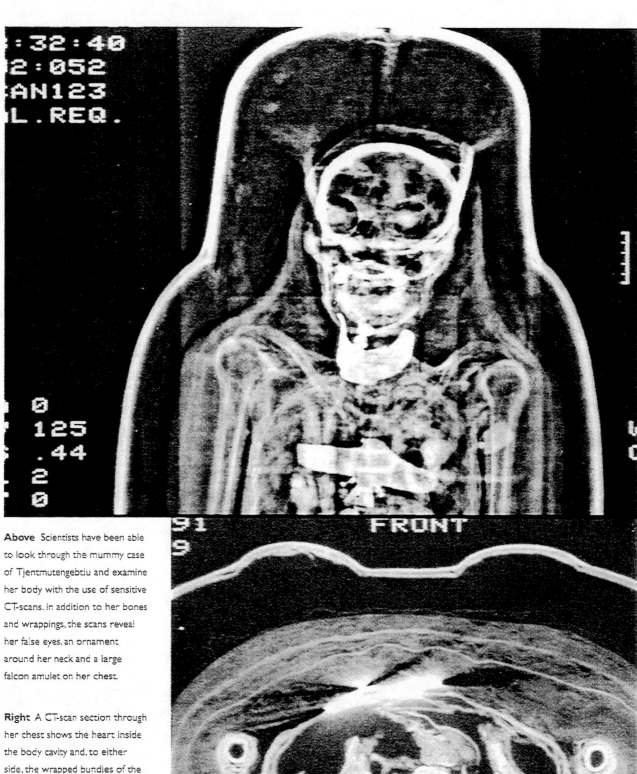

Above Scientists have been able to look through the mummy case of Tjentmutengebtiu and examine her body with the use of sensitive CT-scans. In addition to her bones and wrappings, the scans reveal her false eyes, an ornament around her neck and a large falcon amulet on her chest.

Right A CT-scan section through her chest shows the heart inside the body cavity and, to either side, the wrapped bundles of the individually mummified internal organs, which were returned to the body. The metal falcon amulet resting on her chest appears as a patch of intense white.

A CT-procedure involves the radiographic scanning of the body, from top to bottom, in a series of lateral slices or cross-sections. The data from the scan is stored in a digital format for use in a computer to create a three-dimensional image of any part of the body which can be viewed clearly in isolation and rotated on screen to be seen from any angle. Because the scanner's beams are highly sensitive to the differing densities of structures and objects within the body, bone, soft tissue such as skin or internal organs, embalming substances and other funerary objects such as amulets or papyrus, even wax figurines, can be easily distinguished. As so strikingly shown in the case of Tjentmutengebtiu, the computer can be used to reconstruct on screen a three-dimensional image of the lady's head, showing the linen packing in her cranium and the amount of soft tissue still preserved.

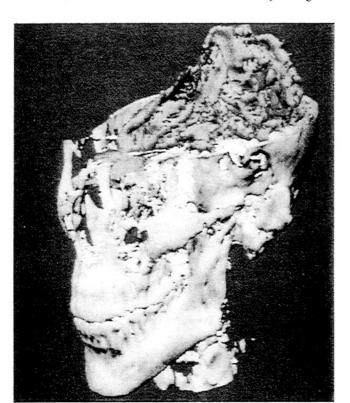

Above The data from the CT-scans can be used to generate a three-dimensional model of any part of the body. Here a cut-away view of Tjentmutengebtiu's skull reveals the linen packing (coloured purple) inserted into her cranium after the removal of the brain.

From conventional X-rays, previously taken, it was estimated that she died sometime between the ages of twenty-five and forty. The highly detailed data recovered from the CT-scan on the state of her teeth and the mineral density of her bones now allows a more precise determination of her age at death at between nineteen and twenty-three years, although the cause of death is still unknown.

Another project, organized by Joyce Filer, a physical anthropologist from the British Museum, has been devoted to the examination of mummies from Egypt's Roman period, dating a thousand years later than Tjentmutengebtiu. Mummies of this period are sometimes fitted with wooden panels decorated with painted portraits of their owners instead of the traditional Egyptian mask. The portraits pose an intriguing question: do they reflect the actual age and appearance of the deceased at or near the time of death, or were they painted at some time prior to that event? The use of CT-scanning has helped to answer this query.

A case in point is one of the most famous of these portrait mummies, that of a man called Artemidorus, dating from about AD 100–120. His portrait represents him in his early twenties, but was this his actual age at death? A recent CT-scan, carried out by a team from the Royal National Throat, Nose and Ear Hospital led by Dr Gus Alusi, indicates that it probably was. Particularly diagnostic for his age is the state of his dental development, especially the wisdom teeth which had not yet erupted. His skeleton, which was not quite fully grown, also indicates that he was a young man at the time of his death.

After having determined that the youthful appearance of the portrait corresponded with the age of its owner, another member of the team, Joao

Right One of the finest examples of its kind, the mummy case of Artemidorus incorporates a portrait of its owner painted in a Roman style, while the gilded decoration over the body reflects the traditional Egyptian hope of resurrection with the god Osiris. From Hawara. Roman Period, AD 100–120.

Above The coffin of Artemidorus enters the CT-scanner under the supervision of David Rawson of the Royal National Throat, Nose and Ear Hospital, London.

Opposite High-resolution radiographic images showing the mummy of Artemidorus within his coffin. The skeleton is complete, with much soft tissue surviving. The internal organs and the brain have been removed.

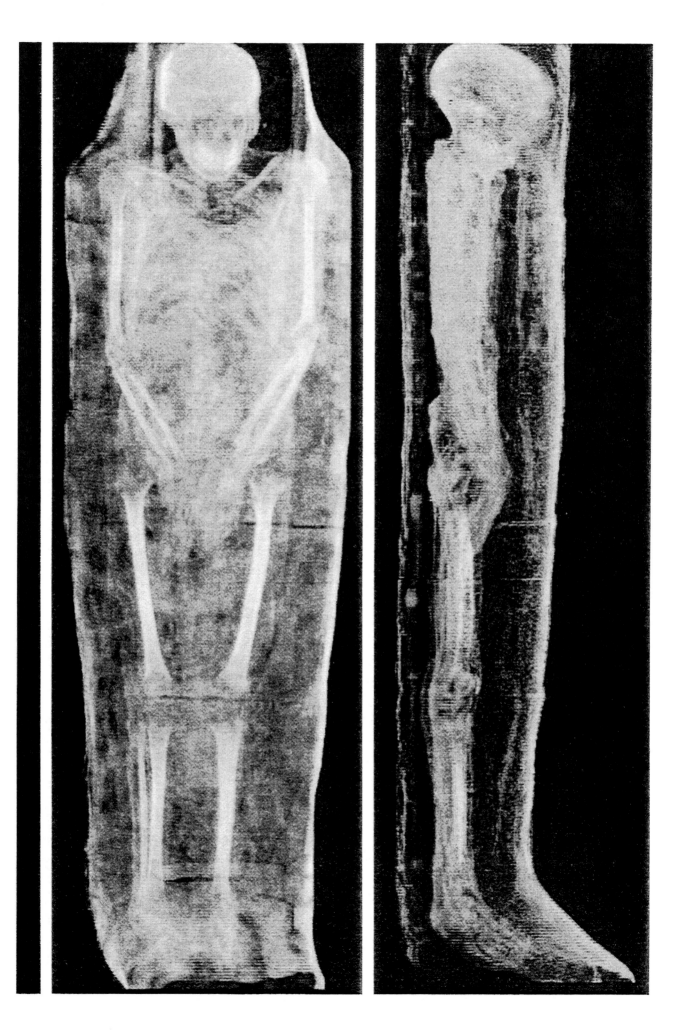

Campos, used the CT-data to see if the handsome likeness mirrored the living reality. To the computer-generated model of Artemidorus' skull, he has added a layer of flesh, using measurements developed in forensic science to help identify anonymous crime victims, appropriately varying in thickness according to the bone structure of the head. After that process is completed, as Campos explains: 'what we do is map the portrait that we've got from the case of the mummy on to the reconstructed face, so we have the real texture of the eyes, eyebrows, lips and skin, and the result is a very realistic view of the face in three dimensions.' The result came as somewhat of a surprise. The true Artemidorus apparently had rather chunky, prominent features, and his striking portrait, although clearly of the same face, was a rather idealized view.

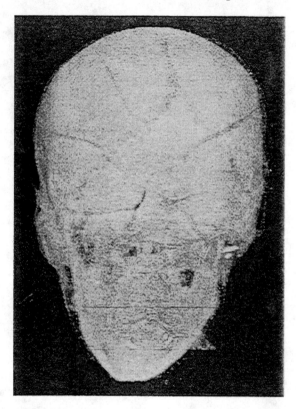

Above Computer reconstruction of the back of Artemidorus' skull, clearly revealing the radiating fractures – the result of a blow by a 'blunt instrument.'

The CT-scan of Artemidorus has revealed another especially intriguing aspect of this young man's life. There is substantial damage to the back of his skull, fractures which Alusi and Filer believe could only have been caused by a 'big blow on the head by a large, heavy object…the proverbial blunt instrument'. Since there are no signs of healing, these injuries, if inflicted on him while still alive, 'must have happened close to the time of death, and may even have been the cause of death'. Further, the number of loose vertebrae and dislocated ribs suggest that the body was already in a state of decomposition when he was mummified. Was Artemidorus the victim of foul play, his body found only sometime later, or simply subjected to rough and careless handling at the embalmer's workshop? Analysis of the scans has not yet been completed, and the final answer to this ancient mystery will have to await the full publication of the project.

It is clear that these new scanning methods can be used to peer through the wrapping of mummies to reveal a wide variety of things, among them details of the craft of the embalmer. The scans have shown us how they did their job, and sometimes how they did not.

Mummification

The process of mummification was held sacrosanct, so the details of exactly how it was done were never publicly recorded by the Egyptians. The earliest written account is by the Greek traveller Herodotus, who visited Egypt in about 450 BC. Over the centuries the techniques of mummification changed considerably, and Herodotus' account can only be used to reflect the customs of his time. According to him, the most expensive method, which involved several stages over a seventy-day period, was well beyond the reach of the ordinary citizen. Later, in the Roman period in which Artemidorus lived, the oils, resins and spices for embalming alone cost 65 drachmas, the equivalent of the average wage for two months' work. The cost of the labour is unknown.

Above At the embalmer's workshop the liver, lungs, stomach and intestines were removed and mummified separately. They were then placed in special containers called canopic jars which were protected by four gods, the Sons of Horus. Even when it became customary to return the organs to the body, canopic jars were still considered necessary equipment, and solid or dummy jars like these wooden ones were made. c. 1000 BC.

At an embalmer's workshop, the body would be laid out. First the brain would be removed through the nostrils with an iron hook and discarded as unimportant. The CT-scan of Artemidorus shows this clearly: to penetrate to the brain, the ethmoid bone, which separates the roof of the nose from the cranial cavity, was broken through, and pieces of this bone and part of the brain can still be seen within the skull. But modern science has shown that this was not the only way: the brain could also be extracted through a hole made at the base of the skull, or even via the eye sockets.

Next, an incision in the abdomen, usually on the left side, was made to remove the internal organs. Here timing was critical. Because of their high water content, internal organs are the first parts of the body to decompose. Modern scans have shown that the skill of the embalmer varied from case to case, but the evisceration of the body was rarely perfect or complete, and organs were frequently left behind. Nevertheless, special care was generally taken to retrieve the liver, lungs, stomach and intestines. These organs were mummified separately by dehydrating them with a naturally occurring salt called natron, a mixture of sodium carbonate and sodium bicarbonate (baking powder). Placed in containers called canopic jars or, as in the case of Tjentmutengebtiu, returned to the body as wrapped parcels, these organs were reunited with the body by magic.

The body was then covered from head to toe with natron, to remove the moisture from the tissue and so prevent decay. The mummy of Artemidorus

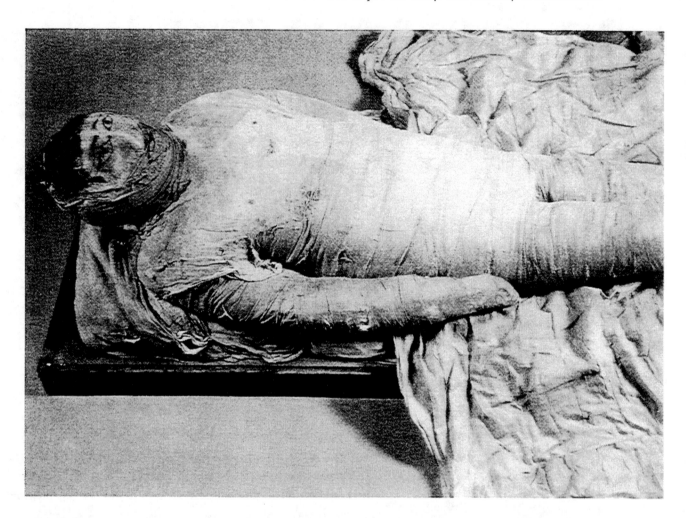

Above One of the oldest preserved mummies, dating from the end of the Fifth Dynasty (c.2400 BC). Huge quantities of linen were used to wrap each individual limb separately. The face is covered with a mask painted directly onto the bandages.

is a fine example of the effectiveness of this treatment, as the scans reveal the preserved state of his ears, nose and probably his tongue. So sensitive are these scans that even the crystals of natron still adhering to his skin can be discerned.

After about forty days the natron was removed and the body washed, and in some cases padded out with linen or sawdust to improve its appearance. Rubbed with oils and coated with resins, it was now ready to be wrapped in linen, sometimes in several hundred metres' worth. One mummy of the early Middle Kingdom, about 2000 BC, had over half a mile (0.75 km) of linen wrappings. The intricate bandaging of the body and the placement of a multitude of amulets within the wrappings could be a time-consuming activity, for aside from lack of vigilance, there is no other explanation for the large

number of insect eggs and small rodents often found beneath the wrappings. Indeed, an elaborate shroud could hide a multitude of sins. For example, while the head of Tjentmutengebtiu had been packed with linen and her body adorned with amulets, for Artemidorus only a small piece of cloth pushed up his nostrils seems to have sufficed to give the appearance that full padding had taken place. This is not the first time modern techniques have revealed a bit of skulduggery on the part of the embalmers.

Artemidorus' mummy contained no amulets of the kind commonly found in earlier Egyptian mummies. It was evidently felt that the funerary scenes depicted on his mummy case sufficed to ensure the afterlife that mummification helped to attain. The fashion in mummy cases and coffins varied widely over time; in Artemidorus' day, while portrait panels were a popular innovation, many still preferred the more traditional funerary mask – one that was gilded if possible, for gold, the flesh of the gods, signified that the deceased

had made it to the afterlife and had become one with the gods. However, attainment of the afterlife was not quite that easy.

The heart, deliberately left in place within the body, was believed to be the source of human personality and the centre of emotions. It was also the key player in the hall of judgement, the last hurdle before entering eternal paradise. Placed on a pan and weighed against the feather of truth, the heart's balance was checked while the deceased proclaimed his or her innocence of forty-two heinous crimes, such as murder, theft or blasphemy. One failure to keep in balance with truth and the heart was eaten by the 'devourer'. Dying this second death was what the Egyptians feared most, and to make sure that it didn't happen, special scarabs made of hard and heavy stone were placed over the heart in the wrappings. Inscribed on the back was a spell, 'Oh, my

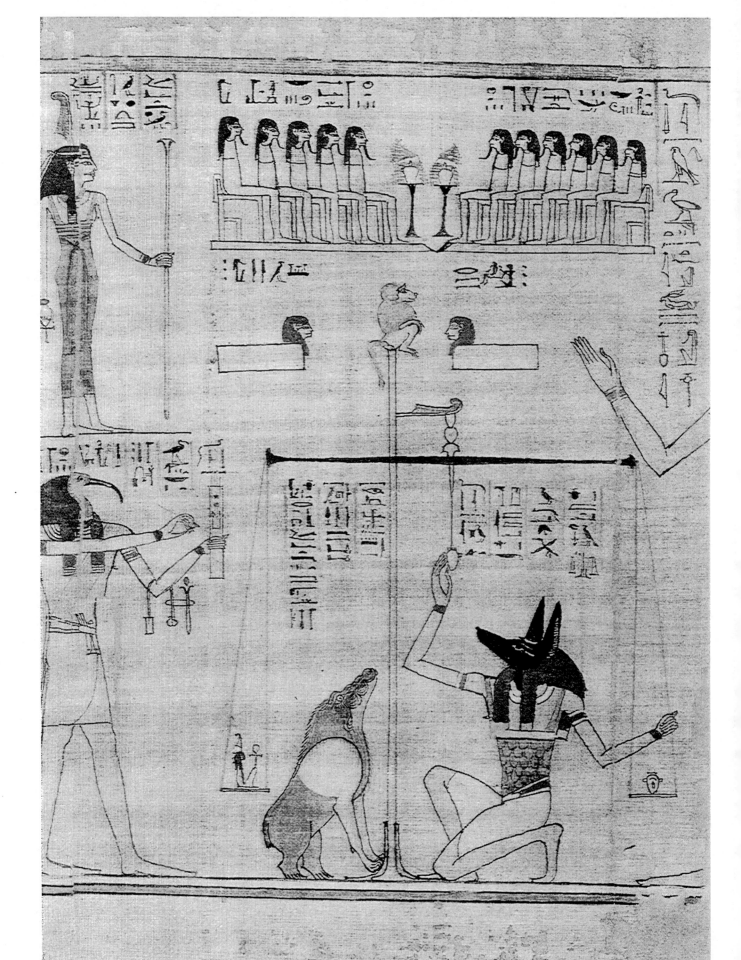

heart which I had from my mother. Do not stand up as a witness against me in the judgement hall…do not tell them what I've really done.'

The most expensive form of mummification, when properly carried out, was undoubtedly very effective. The lifelike remains of the mummified kings of the New Kingdom stand as silent witness to this. They are so well preserved that the sores, possibly of smallpox, are still visible on the face of Ramesses V, the white roots at the base of Ramesses II's dyed red hair can still be seen, and the family resemblance to his father Seti is still quite noticeable.

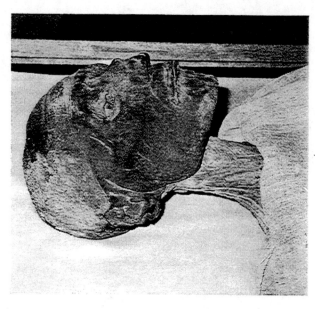

Above The bodies of the kings were treated with the best embalming techniques of their time. The skin of the mummy of Ramesses V is so well preserved that sores, possibly from smallpox, are still visible on his face. Twentieth Dynasty. c.1143 BC.

Opposite Beneath the reed mat, the intact body of a young man was found with linen bandages wrapped around his head and hands. This new discovery at Hierakonpolis suggests that the first step towards mummification had already been taken place in Predynastic times. c.3500 BC.

Origins of Mummification

For the Egyptians, the preservation of the body was essential for the spirit, the *ka*, to find sustenance in the afterlife. Without a body, the spirit would go hungry. It has commonly been thought that this concept was a by-product of the burial customs of the Predynastic Period (*c*.4000 BC), when the dead were placed in shallow graves in the hot, dry sand of the desert, which preserved their bodies naturally. When the graves were disturbed by animals or looters, revealing the nearly lifelike appearance of their ancestors, the Egyptians came to believe that the preservation of the body was important. But as the graves became deeper and more elaborate, partly in an attempt to protect the body from disturbance, the contact with the desiccating heat of the desert was lost and decomposition set in. Thus the practice of mummification was considered to derive from trying to do artificially what hot dry sand did naturally, and by the middle of the First Dynasty (*c*.2950 BC), the date of the earliest preserved artificial mummy, this took the form of wrapping the body in bandages. However, new discoveries at Hierakonpolis in Upper Egypt are revising this view.

In 1997 a team of archaeologists and physical anthropologists under the direction of Dr Renée Friedman of the University of California, Berkeley, began excavating a previously unexplored cemetery at the site of Hierakonpolis. There, about 1 m (3 ft) beneath the desert surface, they found dozens of well-preserved graves of its Predynastic inhabitants, buried in a crouched position and wrapped in matting. Miraculously, these graves had escaped the widespread plundering of the nineteenth century, when cemeteries were pillaged for saleable artefacts and trinkets. This does not mean they had never been disturbed, and it soon became clear that plundering had taken place not long after burial, in the Predynastic Period. The robbers knew exactly who was buried where and what it was they wanted – something evidently located

at the neck. As a result, throughout the cemetery, there had been disturbance to the area of the head, while the remainder of the body was untouched. In some cases, the robbers tunnelled down with such accuracy that only a small slit in the matting at the neck is evidence of their work.

The activities of the grave robbers would certainly have been obvious to the family of the deceased, who would have tried to take preventive measures. What one of these measures may have been became evident with the discovery of two different graves. One was an intact burial of an adult male, aged twenty to thirty-five, who was found still covered in matting and surrounded by seven pots filled with food offerings. As the upper mat was pealed away, the man, who had died at about 3500 BC, emerged. Surprisingly, his head had been wrapped in narrow strips of linen, as were his hands and arms. A similar practice was observed in a heavily plundered burial of a woman, whose long hair was extremely well preserved beneath the linen

Above In the New Kingdom the ceremony to re-animate the mummy, called 'the opening of the mouth' was performed in front of the tomb. While a priest clad in a leopard skin offered incense, several different implements were held to the orifices of the head to restore the senses. Vignette from the papyrus of Hunefer. Nineteenth Dynasty, c.1250 BC.

bandages. In her case, the upper body had been padded with cloth bundles over 10 cm (4 in) thick, perhaps to attain a more life-like appearance. In addition to this padding and wrapping of the body, the surprising discovery of what may be resin on the skin and linen in these and other burials found in this cemetery suggests that, already in Predynastic times, methods of artificial mummification were being tried out, some five hundred years earlier than previously thought. Significantly, the focus of the protective wrapping was the head, essential for identification of the corpse by the spirit, and the hands, the means by which the spirit was fed. This new discovery of Egypt's first mummies suggests that the importance placed upon preserving the body was a concept as old as Egyptian culture itself.

Life and Afterlife

Prior to the funeral, during the period of embalming, the body was considered an empty shell. To re-animate the corpse and restore its senses, a ritual ceremony called 'the opening of the mouth' was performed. During the ceremony, a priest would touch all the orifices of the head with a set of ritual implements. Because these utensils resemble tools used in carpentry, it is thought that the ceremony was originally employed only on statues to animate them with the royal or divine spirit. Already during the first dynasties, however, corpses were revivified in this way. Once restored to his or her senses, the deceased could partake of offerings which were physically present or, from the Old Kingdom onward, magically provided by the myriad of workers depicted on the tomb walls. These tomb paintings depict the deceased as eternally youthful, beautiful and well nourished. The servants, however, were not always so lucky; they could be shown more realistically, suffering from the diseases, deformities and life of toil which their corporeal remains confirm.

The condition of people's bodies can tell us not only how they died but how they lived and to what social class they belonged. Roxie Walker of the Bioanthropology Foundation has for many years been engaged in a study of human remains from excavations in Egypt, part of the research collections of The Faculty of Medicine of the University of Cairo. Among them, two

209

bodies, both female but one belonging to a commoner the other to a queen, form an interesting contrast. Roxie Walker has established that both had died young – one was about twenty, the other eighteen – but had lived very different lives. The anonymous commoner, dating from about 1450 BC, had been involved in manual labour from an early age:

'Her thoracic vertebrae show early arthritic changes due probably to carrying heavy weights. Her arms are robust and show evidence of muscle development indicating that she lifted and carried things. There is substantial wear to the teeth, caused by the standard poor person's diet consisting of coarse bread, onions, vegetables and very little meat.'

The other body is that of a lady named Ashait, one of the queens of Mentuhotep II (2055–2004 BC), the king who founded the Middle Kingdom. It bears no indications of stressful physical activity:

'Her thoracic vertebrae are unmarked by any sign of strain, of effort or of hard work. Her teeth show no wear. There is no evidence for muscular development on her arms, which are long and slender. Her well-preserved hand is gracile and elegant, her nails beautifully manicured and stained red with henna.'

Ashait was a refined lady, who had lived a privileged and pampered life, albeit a short one. Even had we not known her name and circumstances, this much could have been deduced from examination of her body alone.

Above Roxie Walker examines the skull of an anonymous commoner in the museum in the Faculty of Medicine of Cairo University. Social class can often be determined from the study of human remains.

Right The beautiful manicured and henna-dyed nails on the delicate hand of Queen Ashait indicate that she led a life of leisure: c.2020 BC.

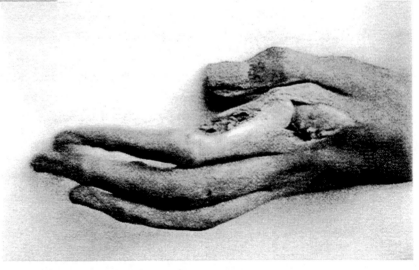

The same collection contains some of the finest examples of human hair to have survived from antiquity. Hair, potentially a rich source of information on a wide range of cutural and medical issues, is a relatively neglected subject. now receiving productive attention from Dr Joann Fletcher of the University of Manchester. By examining hair samples microscopically, for example, she has shown that head lice were common among the ancient Egyptians. Though lice are certainly a health hazard, as they can carry certain diseases and cause skin infections, contrary to popular belief they are not the result of poor hygiene: 'They thrive in clean short hair, where they have easy access to the host's blood supply, feeding several times a day…and the louse is no respecter of class, being quite at home in the hair of pharaohs and farm-

Above Hair is a rich source of information about the ancient Egyptians. Detailed examination by Joann Fletcher of the hair of Hat-nufer, who died about 1450 BC. has shown that the braided plaits are actually extentions that had been woven into the natural greying locks of the elderly lady after her death. These were then fashioned into an elaborate bouffant style such as that worn by the goddess Hathor.

ers alike.' The frequency of lice in fact suggests that the Egyptians washed their hair routinely. To prevent an infestation some relied on regular combing and the use of oils; others shaved their scalps and wore wigs, which also protected their heads from the sun. Ultimately, the way you dressed your hair in public and the kind of wig you wore were significant social markers. The more important you were, the more elaborate the style.

Dr Fletcher's research is shedding especially interesting new light on the question of the colour of hair. She has determined that,

'the wide range of shades portrayed in Egyptian art does, to a large extent, reflect the diverse range found in reality. The most common hair colour, then as now, was a very dark brown, almost black colour. although natural auburn and even (rather surprisingly) blonde hair are also to be found.'

As today, it was commonplace to disguise grey hair with a dye, normally a form of henna. Greying locks could also be hidden with extensions of human hair braided carefully into the owners natural hair. It was a vanity which was not only indulged in life but also extended to the afterlife: hair could be elaborately styled after death, as one would want to look one's best for the most important of all journeys.

Disease

Bones, hair and teeth contain important evidence of lifestyle and of the many afflictions that affected the ancient Egyptians, but many ailments leave no mark on the bone. For determining a wider range of health patterns in ancient Egypt, as well as the ancient Mediterranean world, the tissues preserved in mummies are a unique resource.

Dr Rosalie David, Keeper of Egyptology at the Manchester Museum, has

Opposite The gilded mask of 'Manchester Mummy 1766' indicates that this young woman was from a wealthy family. X-rays suggest that she suffered from a painful parasitic infection, but only a test on tissue sample will confirm this. Roman Period, first–second century AD.

Overleaf Endoscopic examination of Mummy 1766 by the Manchester team, from left to right, Drs David Counsell, Rosalie David, Eddie Tapp and Ken Wildsmith. The results are visualized on the screen on the left. Before and during the procedure, a series of rotating radiographic images which helped to locate the internal organs accurately were taken by the Manchester Royal Infirmary's state-of-the-art multi-sectional X-ray machine, on the right.

been at the forefront of mummy research for many years. Over her career she has investigated a number of the health problems the Egyptians faced, and she is currently interested in tracing the pattern of one disease called schistosomiasis (bilharzia) over a 5000 year period from ancient to modern times. Schistosomiasis is a debilitating and ultimately fatal condition caused by a parasitic worm present in the sluggish waters of irrigation canals. The worm enters the human body by penetrating the skin and grows to maturity in the liver; it then moves to the bladder and intestines to breed, laying thousands of spiky eggs which trigger painful inflammation in its human host. The disease is endemic today in Egypt, and it was probably prevalent in ancient times, but because accurate diagnosis has been dependent on finding the actual remains of the parasite in the liver or intestines (organs often removed in the mummification process), the extent of the disease in ancient times has been difficult to ascertain. However, a new laboratory test recently developed for rapid diagnosis of living patients may be equally useful in diagnosing sufferers long dead. Called the ELISA test, it detects the antigen released by the body into the bloodstream specifically to fight off the schistosomiasis worm.

As a first step toward determining the incidence of this disease in antiquity, Dr David must validate this new test on ancient mummified remains. To do this she has chosen 'Manchester Mummy 1766', the body of an anonymous young woman who died in the first or second century AD. Her gilded mask, covering her head and chest, is adorned with modelled snake-bracelets, rings and necklaces inlaid with glass imitations of semi-precious stones. Although she appears to be a lady from a well-to-do family, unlikely to suffer from such a disease, an X-ray examination of her mummy in 1972 revealed evidence of calcification of the bladder, one of the common results of virulent schistosomiasis infection.

On 2 November 1997 Mummy 1766 was wheeled into the Neuroradiology Department of the Manchester Royal Infirmary for her first test. Here, doctors inserted through an existing hole in the mummy a narrow tube fitted with a miniature camera called an endoscope to guide them in the recovery of tissue samples from deep inside the body. According to Rosalie David, 'the use of the endoscope was a breakthrough, which the Manchester team pioneered back in the mid-eighties, because with it we are virtually non-destructive in our examination of the mummies.' Directed by multi-sectional X-ray images, the endoscope was able to penetrate deeper into the body than ever before and retrieve several uncontaminated samples not only for use in the study of schistosomiasis but also for further research on, among other topics, pain relief.

Dr David Counsell, Consultant Anaesthetist at Victoria Hospital in Blackpool, has had a lifelong interest in ancient Egypt. Combining his passion with his training, he is now investigating the use of pain-relieving drugs in ancient Egypt. He hopes that the samples from Manchester Mummy 1766

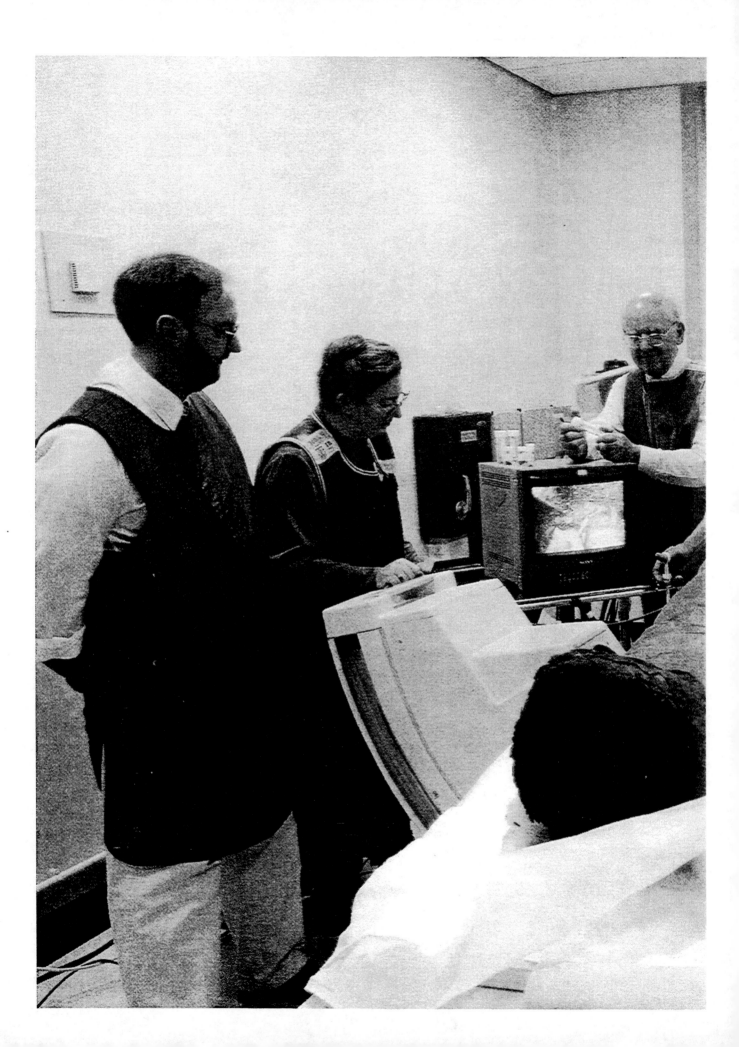

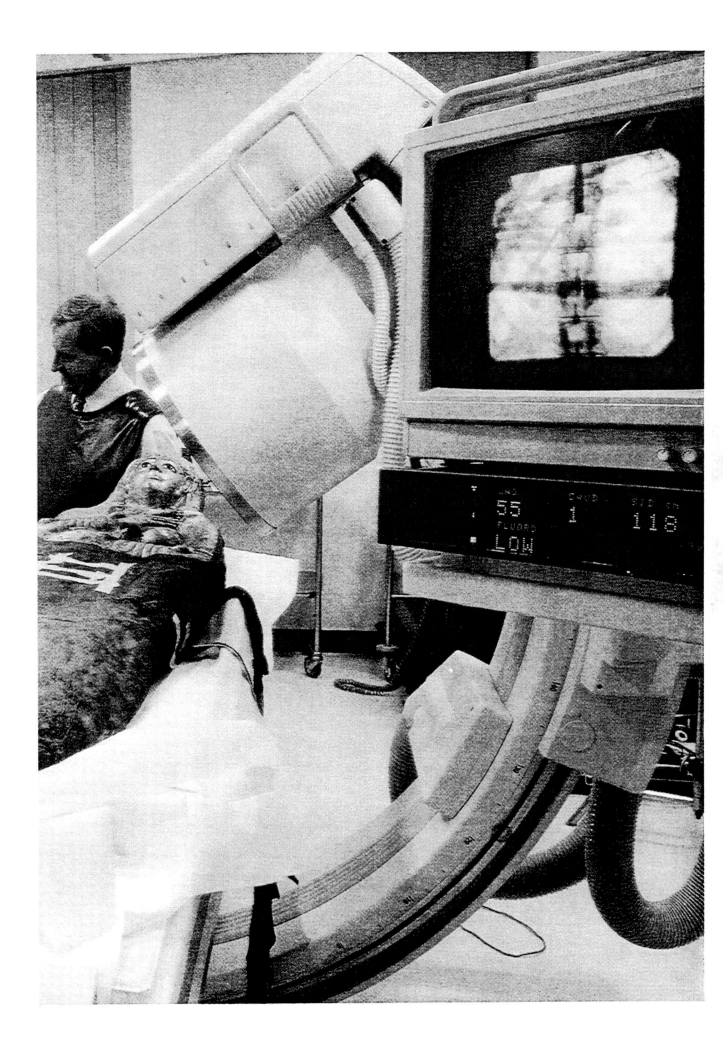

Right The poppy from which the drug opium is derived is not native to Egypt. It is thought, however, that the ancient Egyptians may have imported it from Cyprus, where the flower grows wild, in small juglets that seem to imitate in their form the poppy's seed capsule (right). To date, these jars are the only evidence to suggest the Egyptians used this drug, but new analytic methods may produce scientific proof.

in particular will shed some light on this topic, because the condition of the bladder indicates that the lady must have suffered greatly. As Dr Counsell explains:

> 'We know a lot about the traditions of medicine in ancient Egypt, and we also know that the ancient Egyptians were likely to have known about some of the powerful plant-based drugs the we still use in modern medicine today. We'd be particularly interested in drugs such as morphine and codeine, which are both powerful pain-killers and both derive from the opium poppy. It is quite clear that drugs such as opium were in widespread use at around the time of Christ. There is written evidence describing opium, the harvesting of opium, its use as a pain-killer and indeed its side-effects. But what we don't know is how or if it was used before that time.'

At the Medimass Laboratory in Manchester, a laboratory which specializes in forensic and chemical identification, a minute sample from Mummy 1766 will be analysed using gas chromatography and mass spectroscopy to find out. If any narcotics are present, they will be detected by their mass and weight. These very accurate techniques can also determine if the drugs were actually taken in life and metabolized, or whether they are contaminants or by-products of the mummification process. According to Dr Counsell,

> 'These techniques have been applied in a wide range of archaeological circumstances over the past few years, but I think we've only just scraped the surface of the possibilities that are available…From my own point of view, the important aspect of this work is to push back the boundaries of history.'

But it is not just to satisfy our fascination with the ancient Egyptians that this scientific work is done. Techniques honed in the analysis of Egyptian mummies are now being used to perfect the scanning and evaluation of living patients, saving money and saving lives.

Contribution to Modern Medicine

While new scientific techniques are producing fresh insights, otherwise largely unattainable, into how the ancient Egyptians lived and died, there has also been a reciprocal benefit to modern medicine. Mummies are proving to be valuable 'guinea-pigs' in the refining of techniques before they are used on live human beings.

The CT-scanning of Artemidorus, which yielded so much useful Egyptological information, was part of such a process. Many of the surgical operations carried out at the Royal National Throat, Nose and Ear Hospital, London are targeted on the base of the skull in an area containing major arteries and nerves. Dr Gus Alusi and his colleagues have been investigating ways of eliminating the risk of damaging these delicate structures during surgery and of safely reducing the time required to perform operations in this complex area of the body. Artemidorus has been enormously helpful to the team in achieving the desired end:

> 'One of the more difficult aspects of the research has been actually getting preliminary data of a high enough resolution that we could use for more accurate visualization. The Egyptian mummy, encased and wrapped in bandages, challenged us and provided us with problems that we had to solve in order to be able to see certain parts of the anatomy more accurately... The kind of data required to determine how best to produce optimal quality images could not have been obtained from scans on living patients as it would have meant a very large and potentially lethal dose of radiation.'

The Chantress of Amun, Tjentmutengebtiu, has made an equally significant contribution to modern health, in her case by helping the scientists at St Thomas's Hospital, London to generate an improved and safe method of monitoring difficult pregnancies. After the experience gained in 1992 from calibrating the scanner to electronically unwrap the mummy and examine her internal organs, it occured to Dr Stephen Hughes, 'that the same computer technique, adapted for ultra-sound, could be used to scan babies in the womb, measure their limbs and monitor the growth of their organs'. One of the first young mothers to benefit from this new procedure was Mrs Yolanda Sykes, who had suffered difficulties during a previous pregnancy. But in 1994 she gave trouble-free birth to a healthy boy, Christopher, and expressed her gratitude publicly: 'Knowing problems would be picked up by the scan

Above Mrs Yolanda Sykes and her son
Christopher visiting the mummy of
Tjentmutengebtiu in the British Museum:
'I never thought I'd have cause to be
grateful to someone who had been dead
for 3000 years.'

was great...I never thought I'd have cause to be grateful to someone who had been dead for 3000 years. But we've all got good reason to be thankful to Christopher's other mummy.' Many a mother and child have since had occasion to be thankful to this new technique. Fascinatingly, the Egyptians' quest for rebirth in the next world has helped make possible safe birth in this one.

But the contribution of mummies to modern medicine promises to go well beyond simply playing the role of the guinea-pig. In 1985 the Swedish scientist Dr Svante Pääbo successfully cloned DNA extracted from the tissue of an Egyptian mummy and thereby helped to initiate the brand-new field of 'molecular archaeology'. Ancient Egypt, with its huge quantities of well-preserved human and animal remains spanning several millennia, offers an unparalleled wealth of raw material for palaeobiological studies and has been at the forefront of such research. The unique 'genetic fingerprint' encoded in an individual's DNA offers the prospect of establishing the existence of relationships between one person and another, between one family and another, and between entire populations – information of fundamental historical and demographic importance which cannot be certainly retrieved from any other source. In the field of medicine, molecular archaeology offers the possibility of identifying the ancestors of certain diseases, through the DNA of the relevant pathogen, and of tracing their evolution through time, a process which, experts believe, could assist in the development of antidotes. Hepatitis B and malaria are among several major diseases which have been targeted for such study. To date, ancient DNA research has been beset by methodological difficulties and there is no question that extravagant claims have been made on the basis of flawed or contaminated samples. But as these difficulties are resolved and techniques of retrieval and analysis are improved, more sure progress, and some important breakthroughs, can be expected.

One very popular image of the Egyptian mummy is that of the vengeful monster of the horror movie. In reality, however, mummies are no joke, nor is any curse attached to them. Properly approached and treated, they are eloquent witnesses to the past and rich repositories of scientific information, of potential benefit to the whole of mankind.

FURTHER READING

Adams, B. and Cialowicz, K., *Protodynastic Egypt*, Princes Risborough 1997

Andrews, Carol, *Egyptian Mummies*, London 1984

Andrews, Carol, *Amulets of Ancient Egypt*, London 1994

Andrews, Carol, *Ancient Egyptian Jewellery*, London 1996

Andrews, Carol (ed.), *The Ancient Egyptian Book of the Dead* (trans. by Raymond O. Faulkner), London 1989

Arnold, D., *Building in Egypt: Pharaonic Stone Masonry*, New York 1991

Baines, J. and Malek, J., *Atlas of Ancient Egypt*, Oxford 1980

Bierbrier, M., *The Tomb-Builders of the Pharaohs*, Cairo 1989

Bietak, Manfred, *Avaris: Capital of the Hyksos. Recent Excavations*, London 1996

Bowman, Alan K., *Egypt after the Pharaohs*, London 1996

Capel, Anne K. and Markoe, Glenn E. (eds), *Mistress of the House, Mistress of Heaven: Women in Ancient Egypt*, New York 1996

David, R. and Tapp, E. (eds), *Evidence Embalmed: Modern Medicine and the Mummies of Ancient Egypt*, Manchester 1984

David, R., and Tapp, E. (eds), *The Mummy's Tale: The Scientific and Medical Investigation of Natsef-Amun, Priest in the Temple at Karnak*, London 1992

Davies, W.V., *Egyptian Hieroglyphs*, London 1987

Donadoni, S. (ed.), *The Egyptians*, Chicago 1997

Filer, Joyce M., *Disease*, London 1995

Forman, Werner and Quirke, Stephen, *Hieroglyphs and the Afterlife in Ancient Egypt*, London 1996

Germer, R., *Mummies. Life after Death in Ancient Egypt*, Munich/New York 1997.

Hart, G., *Egyptian Myths*, London 1990

Hawass, Z., *Silent Images. Women of Pharaonic Egypt*, Cairo 1995

Hoffman, M.A., *Egypt Before the Pharaohs: The Prehistoric Foundations of Egyptian Civilization*, revised and updated, University of Texas 1991

Hornung, E., *Idea into Image: Essays on Ancient Egyptian Thought*, New York 1992

James, T.G.H., *Egyptian Painting*, London 1985

James, T.G.H. and Davies, W.V., *Egyptian Sculpture*, London 1983

Kemp, B.J., *Ancient Egypt: Anatomy of a Civilization*, London 1989

Kendall, Timothy, *Kerma and the Kingdom of Kush 2500–1500 B.C.: The Archaeological Discovery of an Ancient Nubian Empire*, National Museum of African Art, Washington 1997

Kitchen, K.A., *Pharaoh Triumphant: The Life and Times of Ramesses II, King of Egypt*, Warminster 1982

Lehner, M., *The Complete Pyramids*, London 1997

Lesko, L.H. (ed.), *Pharaoh's Workers: The Villagers of Deir El Medina*, Cornell University Press 1994

Malek, J., *In the Shadow of the Pyramids: Egypt during the Old Kingdom*, London 1986

Manley, B., *The Penguin Historical Atlas of Ancient Egypt*, Harmondsworth 1996

Moran, W.L., *The Amarna Letters*, Baltimore 1992

Nunn, John F., *Ancient Egyptian Medicine*, London 1996

O'Connor, D., *Ancient Nubia: Egypt's Rival in Africa*, Philadelphia 1993

Parkinson, R.B., *The Tale of Sinuhe and other Ancient Egyptian Poems 1940–1640 BC*, Oxford 1997

Parkinson, Richard, *Voices from Ancient Egypt: An Anthology of Middle Kingdom Writings*, London 1991

Parkinson, Richard and Quirke, Stephen, *Papyrus*, London 1995

Pinch, Geraldine, *Magic in Ancient Egypt*, London 1994

Quirke, Stephen, *Who Were the Pharaohs? A history of their names with a list of cartouches*, London 1990

Quirke, Stephen, *Ancient Egyptian Religion*, London 1992

Quirke, Stephen and Spencer, Jeffrey (eds), *The British Museum Book of Ancient Egypt*, London 1992

Reeves, N., *The Complete Tutankhamun: The King, The Tomb, The Royal Treasure*, London 1990

Reeves, N. and Wilkinson, R., *The Complete Valley of the Kings: Tombs and Treasures of Egypt's Greatest Pharaohs*, London 1996

Robins, Gay, *Women in Ancient Egypt*, London 1993

Robins, Gay, *The Art of Ancient Egypt*, London 1997

Shaw, Ian and Nicholson, Paul, *British Museum Dictionary of Ancient Egypt*, London 1995

Spencer, A.J., *Early Egypt: The Rise of Civilisation in the Nile Valley*, London 1993

Spencer, Jeffrey (ed.), *Aspects of Early Egypt*, London 1996

Stead, Miriam, *Egyptian Life*, London 1986

Taylor, John H., *Unwrapping a Mummy*, London 1995

Taylor, John, *Egypt and Nubia*, London 1991

Verner, M., *Forgotten Pharaohs, Lost Pyramids: Abusir*, Prague 1994

Walker, C.B.F., *Cuneiform*, London 1987

Walker, Susan and Bierbrier, Morris (eds), *Ancient Faces: Mummy Portraits from Roman Egypt*, London 1997

Welsby, Derek A., *The Kingdom of Kush: The Napatan and Meroitic Empires*, London 1996

Wente, E., *Letters from Ancient Egypt*, Atlanta 1990

Wildung, D. (ed.), *Sudan: Ancient Kingdoms of the Nile*, Paris/New York 1997

Williams, Jonathan (ed.), *Money: A History*, London 1997

A number of periodicals provide up-to-date reports on current archaeological fieldwork and research projects. Especially recommended are *Egyptian Archaeology. The Bulletin of the Egypt Exploration Society* (London), *KMT. A Modern Journal of Ancient Egypt* (Sebastopol), and *Sudan and Nubia. The Bulletin of the Sudan Archaeological Research Society* (London). For membership/subscription details, contact respectively The Egypt Exploration Society, 3 Doughty Mews, London WC1N 2PG, UK; KMT Communications, 18 Lucero Road, Santa Fe, NM 87505–8845, USA; and The Sudan Archaeological Research Society, c/o Department of Egyptian Antiquities, British Museum, London WC1B 3DG, UK

INDEX

221

ILLUSTRATION ACKNOWLEDGEMENTS

Ägyptisches Museum und Papyrussamlung, Berlin: 107.

Ashmolean Museum, Oxford: 46, 61.

Manfred Bietak: 120 (below).

Bristol Museum and Art Gallery: 192.

British Museum, London, courtesy of the Trustees of the British Museum:
Contents page (below), 16, 17, 18, 22, 23 (above & below), 28, 32
(casts of original in Cairo Museum), 36 (right), 64, 109 (copy), 110 (below),
111 (below), 119, 137, 138, 149, 152, 155, 170 (above), 172 (above), 175
(below), 176, 180–81, 182, 183 (left and right), 184, 189 (below), 190, 193,
194–5, 198 (right), 201, 203, 204–5, 208–9.

Alfredo and Angelo Castiglione: 132–3, 134.

John and Deborah Darnell: 117, 118 (above and below).

Vivian Davies: 20, 29, 31, 34, 39, 52, 59, 72, 73, 76, 80, 81, 83, 84, 86
(below), 87, 94 (above & below), 96, 100–101, 102, 103, 105, 111
(above: Cairo Museum), 121, 125, 131 (left and right), 134, 136 (below),
151 (Cairo Museum), 168, 185, 188, 189 (above), 191, 198 (right), 206
(Cairo Museum), 218.

Egypt Exploration Society: 186.

Joann Fletcher 210 (below).

Werner Forman Archive, London: 93, 172 (below right), 173.

Renée Friedman: 12, 13 (above & below: Hearst Museum), 40–41, 43
(above), 47, 48, 53 (Hearst Museum), 57, 60, 62 (above), 62 (below: Louvre,
Paris), 63, 65, 68, 71 (Cairo Museum), 86 (above), 90, 112–13, 144–5, 157,
171 (below: Cairo Museum), 172 (below left: Manchester Museum), 175
(above), 177 (right), 212 (Manchester Museum), 216 (Manchester Museum).

German Archaeological Institute, Cairo: 37 (above, centre & below).

Peter Hayman: title page, contents page (above), 10, 14, 15, 44, 50, 51, 91,
97, 98, 110 (above: Luxor Museum), 116, 124 (above and below), 126
(above and below), 127 (Khartoum Museum), 128, 135 (Luxor Museum),
136 (above), 139, 143, 146, 150, 154 (above and below), 155, 156, 158,
160–61, 162, 164, 166, 167 (below), 170 (below), 174, 179, 210 (above),
211.

Hierakonpolis Expedition Archive: 24, 26, 207.

Friedrich Hinkel: 104.

Yarko Kobylecky: 120 (above).

The Manchester Museum, The University of Manchester: 214–15.

Ian Mathieson: 66, 67 (above & below).

The Metropolitan Museum of Art, New York: 108 (above: Purchase,
Edward S. Harkness Gift, 1926 [26.7.1412]), 108 (below: Fletcher Fund,
1926 [26.8.125, 127]), 165 (Rogers Fund and Contribution from
Edward S. Harkness, 1929 [29.3.2]).

Museo Egizio, Turin: 171 (above), 177 (above left and below left), 178, 202.

Royal National Throat, Nose and Ear Hospital, London: 199, 200.

S4C (graphics by 4:2:2 Videographics, Bristol): 19 (above), 27, 33, 42, 43
(below), 78–9, 123.

St Thomas's Hospital, London: 196–7.

Staatliche Sammlung Ägyptischer Kunst, Munich: 106.

Miroslav Verner: 88 (above, centre & below), 89.

Fred Wendorf: 19 (below), 21.